D1290578

PHILOSOPHY IN THE CLASSROOM

Matthew Lipman
Dept. of Philosophy
Montclair State College

Ann Margaret Sharp
Dept. of Educational Foundations
Montclair State College

Frederick S. Oscanyan
Dept. of Philosophy
Yale University

Published for
    The Institute For The Advancement Of Philosophy For Children
    Montclair State College, Upper Montclair, N.J. 07043

Copyright© 1977
by
Matthew Lipman, Ann Margaret Sharp, Frederick S. Oscanyan

Library of Congress No. 76-9319
ISBN 0-916834-04-2

Printed in the United States of America
By Universal Diversified Services, Inc.
West Caldwell, N.J. 07006

TABLE OF CONTENTS

PHILOSOPHY IN THE CLASSROOM

Table of Contents

CHAPTER SEVEN: Logic for Children

CHAPTER EIGHT: Can Moral Education be Divorced from Philosophical Education?

Chapter One

MIND

AND THE

CURRICULUM

1. THE CHILD'S HUNGER FOR MEANING

There is rather general agreement that children with reading problems are also likely to be hampered in their thinking. Improving the way such children read, it is believed, will likely improve the way they think.

But it is our contention that reading and thinking are interdependent. Each ministers to the other. Consequently, helping children think can very well result in helping them to read.

The concern about children's reading should not be shrugged off as an anxiety about something superficial or unimportant. If reading and thinking are interdependent, there is reason to be concerned if it should actually be the case that children are far less proficient in reading than they could be or if even competent readers seem to care little about reading.

Now, what motivates children to read? What's the incentive? What do they get out of it?

No answer to these questions is more plausible than that one reads to get meanings. If we try to read a book and become more and more convinced that it is meaningless, we throw it aside. The child does the same thing. Children who can't find meaning in what they read simply stop reading.

But what kind of meanings do children look for?

Surely not just any old meanings. Surely the meanings they're hungry for are those that might be relevant to—and that might illuminate—their lives. Some of these problems are unique to the stage of growth through which they happen to be passing. Others are problems common to all human beings. Children wonder about both sorts of problems. They wonder why they're expected to obey rules and customs, and they wonder about their own identities. They wonder why they're expected to go to school every day, they wonder how the world began, and how it might end. Sometimes they may wonder what to do about their own appetites and emotions.

Children are often reluctant to talk about their problems—they often have a sense of discretion and privacy which we must respect. But many such children would still like to engage in discussions where problems like their own might come up. For example, take what the jargon of psychology identifies as "sibling rivalry." Many times, children in the same family who aren't getting along with one another will be unable to discuss these conflicts with each other. But they'll love to read fairy tales about sister princesses who don't get along, or about princes in the same royal family who are rivals for parental affection. Somehow, it takes the sting out of the problem when it can be understood as part of a story that begins with, "Once upon a time ..." In the make-believe setting of the fairy tale, the problem of sibling rivalry can be considered more detachedly, just as Homer helped the Greeks see themselves more objectively in his great portrait of their war with Troy.

So, if children are to develop a sustained interest in reading, it must be meaningfully relevant to their major concerns—to the things that matter most to them in their lives. What counts is not just learning to see words and say them, but learning to grasp the meanings of words, phrases, sentences, in the contexts in which they appear.

Beginning readers have to learn to find connections—connections which are often extremely difficult to pinpoint. It's not just what a sentence *says* that's important. What does it suggest? What does it imply?

For example, suppose a mother says to you about one of your students: "Oh, I'll admit he's not very good in *spelling*!" What is she suggesting? Isn't she hinting that spelling's not all that important anyway, but that her son's quite good in certain other subjects?

Or take a statement like, *"Everyone's* going to the party!" Taken literally, it could mean merely that "everyone's going, so I'm going too." But it may also be taken as suggesting that everyone "who counts," everyone "who's anyone" is going. Or, accompanied by tears, it may mean, "everyone else is going, so why can't I?"

To discover meanings in written passages, a child has to be sensitive to meaning, and has to know how to *infer* it or draw it out. Inference is reasoning from what's given literally to what's suggested or implied. If someone says "Oh, you're Norwegian, so you must like snow!" you should be able to infer that he's assuming that all Norwegians like snow. If you read that "only women are excluded from the club," you can legitimately infer that all men are admitted. Or, if you know that today is Tuesday the 14th, you shouldn't have much trouble inferring that tomorrow will be Wednesday the 15th.

At every moment of our lives, we draw inferences. If you're crossing the street and hear a horn, you infer a car is coming. If you see an empty glass coated with milk on the inside, you infer that someone has had a glass of milk. Thanks to inference, we can draw a myriad of meanings from what we see, hear, taste, touch and smell, as well as from what we think.

Naturally, the more readily children can draw inferences, the more meanings they'll be able to extract from what they read. This in turn should make their reading more satisfying. And the more satisfied they are by what they read, the more often they're likely to read— whether for entertainment, for comfort, or for understanding.

2. HOW DO CHILDREN LEARN TO REASON?

No one knows for sure how they do it, but thinking is so intimately connected with language that it is widely suspected that learning to speak, learning to think and learning to reason are all tied in with one another. It could well be that part of the explanation of how children learn to reason is to be found in observing how they learn to talk.

Certainly the child's achievement in learning to organize words into grammatical sentences is utterly magnificent. That this feat is performed every day by children all over the world, in every imaginable language, is one of the most extraordinary facts we know. It's not only the learning of words that is so remarkable, but organizing them as they are spoken into grammatically correct structures—and this by virtual infants! The relating of thoughts to one another logically, as well as grammatically, is yet another striking achievement.

Evidently children bring with them these dispositions to organize their thinking and speaking grammatically and logically. But just as children must be taught the difference between using language well and using it badly (e.g., ungrammatically), so they must be taught the difference between reasoning soundly and reasoning sloppily.

We spend a great deal of time helping children see the difference between well-constructed and badly-constructed prose, or between properly executed and improperly executed exercises in arithmetic, but we hardly devote any time at all to teaching children to tell better reasoning from worse. And this isn't because children don't need to know how to reason, or lack the ability to learn it. It's because we ourselves are generally unacquainted with logic, and are embarrassed to admit we have so much difficulty in understanding it.

We've been saying that one reason children can't read better than they do is that we don't teach them reasoning. And without reasoning, they can't figure out what they're reading.

Now reading, of course, is the focus of much attention at the present time. Critics accuse the schools of not teaching reading well, and many schools respond by paying greater and greater attention to reading— but often at the expense of other educational objectives.

It's odd, how reading has become an end in itself. There was a time when it was considered simply a means. Parents wanted their children to grow up to be intelligent adults; to develop the child's intelligence, what better means could there be than reading? But increasingly the stress is on reading, while the thinking processes it was supposed to build are neglected. We "redouble our efforts, having forgotten our aims."

It may seem strange that we urge the teaching of reasoning to improve children's reading, and that we urge that reading be seen in turn as a means to helping children think, rather than as an end in itself. We reply that reasoning and reading are skills that can be taught, and that reinforce each other. Whether thinking can be taught is very debatable. But it certainly can be encouraged. And instruction in the procedures of reasoning can be very helpful in developing the art of thinking.

But how is reasoning taught?

Schools often maintain that they are already doing it, and doing it well. To justify their claims, they cite mathematics and language arts programs. Now, arithmetic and reading can contribute usefully to good thinking. But by themselves, they are insufficient. The fact that Johnny adds, subtracts, multiplies, divides, and can race through comic books— or even *Stuart Little*—doesn't mean he can reason clearly. It doesn't mean he's developing habits of efficient thinking, or of arriving at independent judgments. Something more is needed.

In our own program, we try to sensitize children to sloppy thinking at the same time that we try to help them think well. We give them examples like these:

4

"My father's been reading in the papers that smoking causes cancer, so he says he's going to give up reading."

"Whenever I see Elinor, I ask her what she thinks of Joe, and she gets real embarrassed. Boy, does she have a crush on me!"

"I've been told that one child out of every five that's born in the world is Chinese; I have three brothers, so I figure the next baby in our family will probably look pretty Oriental."

Or we ask them absurd questions such as these:

"When is a straight line crooked?"

"Why are dolphins such stupid fish?"

"Is it warmer in the summer or in the city?"

Children can easily learn to spot the flaws in examples like these. But they need to discuss what is wrong under the supervision of someone trained to distinguish between thinking effectively and thinking confusedly.

Obviously, we need to develop attractive ways of presenting matters of intellectual quality without compromising the integrity of the subject. Our objective should not be to confront children with two isolated entities—the structure of logical thought on the one hand, and the urgent and bewildering problems of life on the other. What we must do is allow children to discover how delightfully and how fruitfully thought can play on its subject-matter. We must help them see how reasoning about matters of importance to them can be satisfying to them. At times such reasoning can be inspiring, even if it does no more than reformulate the basic issues more insightfully.

3. THE CHILD AND THE EDUCATIONAL ESTABLISHMENT

So parents turn to the schools for the kind of training that will produce reasoning children. Surely, parents tell themselves, if reasoning is so important, it's taught in the schools.

Unfortunately, this isn't so. Not because of any inability on the part of children to learn the subject, but because of the inability of most teachers to teach it. And why are they unable to teach reasoning? Because they themselves were never taught it!

Indeed, this must be one of the most paradoxical characteristics of our culture: the acquisition by adults of an *incapacity* not generally found in children. The indisposition of adults to learn reasoning contrasts so sharply with the readiness of children to learn it (along with language) that we must face the fact that getting older is in some respects not growth but diminishment.

5

We are dealing here with a breakdown in the transmission of skills from one generation to the next. How could this have happened? Certainly the temptation is to indict the schools for their failure to teach reasoning in any systematic fashion. (In fact, the *mental* life of human beings is largely ignored in the elementary school curriculum, as though our thoughts and their interconnections were in no way a fit subject for children to study.) Yet it would be unfair to blame schools without at the same time indicting other groups and institutions which are no less accountable. Among these, we should especially mention the heavy responsibility of those who construct and publish curricula. Teachers are limited by their materials, and when the materials are deficient, the teacher cannot always compensate for that deficiency.

We often make this problem still worse by offering children with reading difficulties materials even blander and more superficial than those offered to other children. All we do, of course, is compound the problem by giving the child with the problem less and less incentive to solve it.

In challenging children to think, the philosophy for children program also motivates them to read. Significant reading improvements have been reported as a result of the use of the program. Some of the changes in reading performance, under controlled experimental conditions, have been breathtaking. One fifth-grade class, after a four-month trial of the program as taught by their regular teacher, improved 16 months in reading age. Another class, at sixth-grade level, but reading only at 3.5 level, jumped the remaining 2.5 years that brought them up to the national norms, after just that one-semester course!

So philosophy for children can improve reading. It can get dramatic results, and measurable results. As the program improves, and as it stretches from kindergarten through 12th grade, the results should be even more dramatic, and *no less measurable.*

4. WHAT CAN PHILOSOPHY DO FOR CHILDREN?

One of the major problems in the practice of education today is the lack of unification of the child's educational experience. What the child encounters is a series of disconnected, specialized presentations. If it is language arts that follows mathematics in the morning program, the child can see no connection between them, nor can he or she see a connection between language arts and the social studies that follow, or a connection between social studies and physical sciences.

This splintering of the school day reflects the general fragmentation of experience, whether in school or out, which characterizes modern life. However, it is also due to the enormous increase in the factual dimension of human knowledge, for insofar as education involves a transmission of information to the child, it must be simplified and schematized by specialists. The result is that each discipline tends to become self-contained, and loses track of its connections with the totality of human knowledge, in an effort simply to present a bare outline of that particular field.

Since such specialization is likely to prevail for the foreseeable future, there needs to be some way of establishing continuity among the different disciplines that make up the school curriculum. Normally, the burden of establishing continuity is laid upon the teacher, who unfortunately is seldom trained to see continuity between different subject areas. Thus to expect the teacher to be able to establish such continuity for the child is unreasonable. The teacher may not have been trained to be aware of the formal resemblances between grammar, mathematics and logic; or to be aware of the methodological continuities that connect the physical and social sciences; nor can the teacher necessarily see the connections between the literary description of social life and the sociological descriptions of social life. Furthermore, it is unrealistic to ask the teacher to create the continuity between the different subject areas for children when specialists have for so long been unable to organize and express such continuity.

Ultimately there will have to be a recognition by each discipline of its connections with the other areas of human knowledge. There is no good reason why every specialized curriculum should not contain bridges to the other disciplines which will enable the child to confront the interconnections of human knowledge as a fact rather than as a piously hoped-for ideal.

But the immediate step to be taken is to lift the burden of establishing continuity from the teacher and transfer it, at least in part, to the child. This can be done by building upon children's natural curiosity, their natural desire for wholeness, their natural inclination to continue questioning until they are satisfied, whether such inquiry on their part stays within the bounds of prescribed disciplines or not. Children have the motivation and the interest to insist that their understanding be unified and complete. What both children and teacher therefore need is guidance from the curriculum that would indicate to them how to make the connections that they are looking for.

The question arises — how can philosophy satisfy this need for continuity for both teacher and children? The answer seems clear: if children's chief contribution to the educational process is their inquisitiveness, and if philosophy is characteristically a question-raising discipline, then philosophy and children would seem to be natural allies. What could better connect children with the formal structure of human knowledge than a discipline that has traditionally

7

concerned itself with the interrelationship among the different intellectual disciplines, and with the raising of ever more penetrating questions about how human experience is to be understood and interpreted?

In other words, philosophy encourages the intellectual resourcefulness and flexibility which can enable children and teachers alike to cope with the disconnectedness and fragmentization of existing curricula. Its traditional concerns with ethics, with the nature of knowledge and with the nature of reality are concerns that transcend existing disciplines and at the same time are basically related to the subject matters with which existing disciplines deal.

The peculiarity of philosophy is that the questions it raises deal with the nature of human knowledge in a way that is, so to speak, directly at right-angles with the distribution of non-philosophical subject matters. That is, following the accepted division of knowledge into such academic subject matters as physical science, life science, mathematics, history, etc., children are encouraged to ask such questions (if they are encouraged to ask questions at all) as, "What is colonialism?. What is gravitation? What is long division?"

A philosopher, on the other hand, raises questions that are metaphysical, epistemological, aesthetic, or ethical, and what is unique about these questions is that they cut directly across the diverse subject matter areas. To ask what is ethical is to ask a question that applies equally to the sciences, the arts, the professions and every other aspect of human activity. Likewise, every subject matter area has an aesthetic dimension, an epistomological dimension, a metaphysical dimension. The mathematician may insist that children begin by learning simple arithmetical operations, but the children may stagger the teacher by asking, "What is number?" — an immensely profound metaphysical question. The teacher of history may wish to concentrate on the history of the Roman Empire, but the children, with seeming innocence, may first want to know "what is history?" and are duly suspicious of proceeding without an explana-tion. Similarly with such questions as "What is an explanation?", "What is obedience?", "What is goodness?". The teacher who insists that students "get the facts" should be willing to engage in discussion with the child who asks, "But, what is a fact?" In other words, every time children call into question the fundamental assumptions of the subject matter they are studying, they raise metaphysical questions. Everytime they want to know how they can be sure of anything, they are raising epistomological questions. Every time they want to know why, on what grounds, their parents or teachers recommend, say, Tom Sawyer over James Bond, they are raising aesthetic questions.

Now, of course, there is a good deal of controversy as to what

8

answers you give to the question, "What is number?," or "What is a fact?" Nor are we altogether clear what history is, or what an explanation is, or what the mind is, or what human individuality is. In fact, philosophy involves precisely this perpetual effort to come to grips with questions which permit no simple solution and which require continual rephrasing and reformulation. But the fact that there are no ready answers to these philosophical questions which children continually raise is no justification for dismissing such questions when the child asks them. Such questioning represents children's search for wholeness and completeness, their healthy disregard of artificial categories and barriers to understanding. Not to encourage and nurture children's search for comprehension by systematically introducing them to philosophical dialogue through which their curiosity can be nourished and their insights clarified, is to compel them to accept the aridity of the overspecialized view of knowledge as presently found in the schools, rather than the rich, synoptic, comprehensive philosophical view which their questions suggest they prefer.

The 'philosophy for children' approach thus involves the view that children's questions tend to be extraordinarily sweeping in scope and grandeur. To ask a question, "How did the world begin?," or "What is everything made of?," or "What happens to a person when he dies?," is to raise issues of enormous metaphysical import. The fact that children can raise such questions indicates that they begin with a thirst for holistic explanations, and it is patronizing, to say the least, that we should not try to help them develop concepts equal in generality to the questions they ask. Philosophy is therefore of enormous benefit to any individual seeking to form concepts that can effectively represent aspects of his life experience. The teacher who recognizes and respects the sense of totality which children demand will endeavor to help them develop the greatest possible intellectual flexibility and resourcefulness. Children will respect the teacher who takes their questions seriously, even if this means no more than answering a question with another question. Thus, if the child asks, "Is the world made of matter?," the teacher may ask the child, "What do you think matter is?" Or if the child asks, "How did the world begin?," the teacher may ask, "How can you tell that it had a beginning?" This forces the teacher into a role of questioner or searcher like that of the child.

To be asked by a child, "What is death?," is to be compelled to ask oneself what is life. To be asked by a child, "What is mind?," is to be compelled to ask oneself what matter is. In other words, every question that implies a onesided, partial view of things requires an answer that is more exhaustive, and looks at the matter through a richer and more varied set of perspectives.

9

In summary, it is commonplace to deplore the fragmentation and over-specialization that seems to be endemic in education. It is now becoming clear that the solution to this problem will not come from those who are themselves practitioners of these very specializations, because they are themselves already too overspecialized to devise a solution. On the other hand, it is impractical to thrust the burden of generalization and continuity upon teachers who have not themselves been trained to raise the more general questions or to see continuities among the various subject matters. Philosophy in the classroom must be seen as a countervailing force to the over-specialization rampant in the educational system, and the burden of introducing philosophy into the classroom will be borne more than willingly by the children themselves, since the meanings philosophy represents are among those the children cherish most. Obviously, the future of philosophy in the classroom is dependent upon the training of teachers not only to understand the philosophical dimension of children's subject areas that the teacher presently teaches during the school day, but also to learn how systematically to nurture and sharpen (and not merely to tolerate) this philosophical quest on the part of students.

Those who decry the over-specialization of the curriculum have been hard put to come up with a suitable alternative. Proponents of "General Education" have often been able to devise nothing more than monstrous survey courses, a massing of facts from all disciplines thrown together so as to be indigestible. Such an enterprise is pointless. Children need comprehensiveness and a sense of perspective. But they can only develop these if the educational process itself challenges their imagination and gives scope to their intellectual processes while at the same time provides the pathways by which the various subject matters of the curriculum can be integrated with one another. These are two essential requirements for a general education program, and philosophy for children can satisfy both. It provides children with the intellectual and imaginative tools they need, and it provides the mode of transition from subject matter to subject matter that bridges and connects the various disciplines to which the child is exposed during the course of the school day.

Exposure to both the content and the methodology of philosophy is important if the child is ever to develop a frame of reference in which to view the other disciplines to which one is exposed daily, as well as to establish a fluid set of values about oneself and one's relationship to other people and to the world. Traditionally, this was the very role of philosophy, to supply such a unifying basis to education, centered in the beliefs and views of the individual constantly reflecting upon experience. It is this frame of reference that is missing from education today, and thus the tools that the child needs to develop a critical stance towards science, social studies and humanities is lacking. At the same time, the frame of reference essential to understanding the interconnectedness of all knowledge, and the necessity to come to one's own views about the value of the knowledge to which one is exposed is also lacking. It is just this unifying frame of reference that can help a child understand the methodology underlying the different disciplines, and eventually come to the point where he or she can evaluate whatever it is that the discipline elects to perpetuate. Without this understanding, a critical stance becomes impossible, and children remain pawns of the information with which they are presented day after day. To the extent that philosophy presents a range of alternative views about values, meaning and knowledge itself, it liberates children from the dogmatism of ignorance, outlines relative considerations that have been developed, and encourages that "thinking for oneself" which is so much the mark of a truly educated person.

Further, in regard to the training of teachers to encourage philosophical thinking, it is the exposure to and involvement with the history of philosophical ideas that enables a prospective teacher to develop an appreciation for philosophical questioning himself. This sensitivity is essential if one is even to *hear* the philosophical significance of what children say. If one cannot hear the philosophical dimension, then it is inconceivable to expect the teacher to aid children in coming to a deeper awareness of it themselves. It is one thing to be adept at interpreting what children say on a logical, psychological or sociological level and helping them to develop their awareness within these limits; it is quite another thing to appreciate the philosophical dimension of what is being said and systematically aid children to come to their own views about matters of concern to them. Many a young child has begun to inquire and speculate philosophically regarding the nature of knowledge or human morality, only to be diverted to another area because a teacher did not know how to handle the topic in a relevant way. It is the exposure to the questions themselves, as well as the range of alternative answers, that develops the ability to help children become aware of the meaning of their own questions and the range of alternatives that are present to them.

In addition, it is just this exposure that develops in the prospective teacher a skill in dialogue and a fostering of openness and willingness to engage in inquiry — traits that are indigenous to the philosophical activity. These very traits are also essential if meaningful learning is going to occur in any subject area in a classroom. It is insight into the complexity of philosophical issues and their relation to all of knowledge that helps a teacher to realize that there are no absolute answers and that each individual becomes free by developing the necessary tools to find his own answers and the emotional maturity to

11

be willing to revise those answers when new data appears that must be accounted for. This insight can be the basis for a new role of the teacher in the classroom. Rather than a source of answers and information, prospective teachers can begin to view themselves as co-learners, co-searchers for more sufficient and comprehensive answers, always willing to listen to anyone ("even a child") who might have fresh and original insights about human concerns. The teacher then becomes a philosophical model for the children in the classroom which confirms the children in their freedom to think for themselves, to create new and fresh alternatives when confronted with problems of prime importance for themselves and all individuals. Rather than assuming a passive role in the acquisition of knowledge, children begin to sense the intrinsic worth and excitement involved in assuming an active role in the mystery of knowledge, not as an end in itself, but as a tool in coming to more comprehensive answers about the relationship of themselves to the world. They begin to sense that knowing is not just an individual project but a project to be shared with one's classmates and one's teacher, and that together they can be co-searchers for meaning — and once found this new meaning can make a difference in their immediate lives.

It is this atmosphere of openness, dialogue and intrinsic respect for one another's views and potentials, coupled with a lack of dogmatism, which only a teacher can create in a classroom, and which can be so instrumental in making possible meaningful learning for all involved. This atmosphere, coupled with a willingness to explore very real concerns of children about their lives and their problems in a manner which insures the child's mastering the tools of reasoning essential for dealing with these issues, can only have a beneficial effect on the educational process itself.

Chapter Two

PHILOSOPHY:

THE LOST DIMENSION

IN EDUCATION

1. PHILOSOPHY BEGINS IN WONDER

As adults, we have learned to accept the perplexities that emerge from our daily experience, and to take them pretty much for granted. Many of us no longer wonder why things are the way they are. We have come to accept parts of life as puzzling and enigmatic because that is the way they have always been.

Many adults have ceased to wonder because they feel that there is no time for wondering, or because they have come to the conclusion that it is simply unprofitable and unproductive to engage in reflection about things that can't be changed anyhow. Many adults have never had the experience of engaging in wondering and reflecting which somehow made a difference in their lives. The result is that such adults, having ceased to question and to reach for the meanings of their experience, eventually become examples of passive acceptance which children take to be models for their own conduct.

Thus the prohibition against wonder is transmitted from generation to generation. Before long, children now in school will themselves be parents. If we can somehow preserve their natural sense of wonder, their readiness to look for meaning and their hunger to understand why things are the way they are, there might be some hope that at least this upcoming generation will not serve as models of unquestioning acceptance to their own children.

At every moment of a child's life, events impinge upon that child which are perplexing or enigmatic. Consider a small girl from the very moment she wakes up. Perhaps she discovers her mother is angry with her and she is not aware of having done anything to deserve this anger. She is bewildered. On her way to school, she may observe many more things whose meanings are obscure to her: the firehouse flag is at half-mast, garbage cans rolling around the street, some children she knows are walking away from school rather than towards it, one of the street corners is flooded with water, a merchant is opening a series of locks to his store, and so on. Perhaps if she were an adult who, from the moment she woke up, would be willing to take the time to answer the questions that each of these incidents might provoke, the child would gradually begin to piece together some larger understanding of how the world works. In so far as an education aims at providing young people with such an understanding, its greatest resource is the child's perpetual curiosity.

Things are wonderful when we can think of no way of explaining them. It may be a magician's card trick, or a caterpillar turning into a butterfly, or a Schubert trio. It may be a quasar in outer space, or it may be the activities of a virus under a microscope. But whatever it is, if we find it inexplicable, we are inclined to call it marvellous, and wonder at it.

When we find the world wonderful, it's because we seem to be confronted not by soluble problems, but by utter mysteries. You may know ever so much about heredity, but it matters little when you step before the mirror and confront your face. Ah, now there's a mystery! Where did it come from? How did it get to be the way it is? To what extent are you responsible for it? Surely questions like these have occurred to you from time to time.

They occur to children constantly. Because children wonder not only about themselves, but about the world. Where did it come from? How did it get to be the way it is? To what extent are we responsible for it? And if not we, then who?

Children look at their fingernails, and wonder where they came from. How does something like a fingernail grow out from one's body? But then, everything about their body seems fascinating to them.

Likewise, a snail is fascinating to them—or a mud puddle—or the

14

dark spots on the face of the moon. It is only gradually that a crust or scale will grow over their minds, and they will take these things more and more for granted, until from marvelling at everything, they marvel at nothing.

2. WONDER AND MEANING

To explain something, and thus dispel our puzzlement, we must somehow find the surrounding circumstances that might explain it, the conditions accountable for it. Or we must find a context or frame of reference to which the puzzling thing belongs, for we can understand it if it is a meaningful part of a larger whole.

For example, suppose you had planned to go to a movie with some friends, but you got there late—just in time for the last scene, by which you were completely bewildered. So you turn to your friends, as the lights come up, and you say, "What did it mean? What did it mean?" They tell you all that had happened before your arrival—and suddenly the last scene snaps into place. Its meaning becomes clear to you as you see it as a part in a larger whole.

But suppose you hadn't been late at all. Suppose you'd been on time, and had seen the whole film with your friends. But you found the film an enigma from beginning to end, so you turn to your friends and ask, "What did it mean?" Unfortunately, there's not much they can tell you. You saw the whole film, and there's no larger framework to put it in. In this sense, all you can do is try to understand it on its own terms, lacking as it does the larger context that would give it meaning.

Since children do not have a fully-formed frame of reference into which to place each experience as it happens, each such experience takes on for them an enigmatic, puzzling quality. No wonder, then, the children wonder at the world.

Now, there are three ways that children try to cope with the mysteries or marvels they find around them.

The first way is through a scientific explanation. The second way is through a fairy tale or story which offers a helpful interpretation on a symbolic level. The third way by formulating the matter philosophically—in the form of a question.

a. *Scientific Explanation*

The scientific approach usually appeases the child, but if the explanation offered is only partial, the child's appetite for understanding will hardly be satisfied. "Why's there that rainbow on the surface of the puddle?," you're asked. "Because there's a film of oil on the water," you reply. The child may say no more. But the puzzlement can remain. What has oil got to do with rainbows? Why should one

15

cause the other? You've not really dealt with the problem for him; you've merely postponed it.

Nor is there really anything wrong with what you've done. You can destroy a child's curiosity by overkill. You want to help children find out as much as they need to know about the problem they're presently dealing with, without damaging their curiosity itself by telling them more than they want to know.

There are those who say that small children aren't interested in getting scientific explanations—that is, explanations in terms of causes. Children, it is claimed, want to know the *purpose* behind everything, not just the cause.

And surely this is often the case. You may observe to a two-year old how pretty the sky is, and she may reply, "Yes—who painted it?" She sees things made to be pretty, and concludes— by analogy—that the sky must have been made for the same purpose. Pretty things are made by people who paint. The sky is pretty. It must have been painted by someone. So she reasons.

But it would be a mistake to assume that children who ask for explanations necessarily want them in terms of purposes rather than causes. Suppose, for example, the same little girl were to ask you why a cantaloupe has those lines on it. And suppose you decide to tease, so you say, "That's to show us where to cut the slices." But she may not take it as a joke at all. She may take it quite seriously. Small children can *reason*, as Shulamith Firestone has argued, but they're painfully short on *information* and experience. The fact that the child believes you doesn't mean she wanted an answer in terms of the *purpose* of the lines on the cantaloupe; it may simply mean that she isn't yet able to distinguish between explaining by causes and explaining by purposes. But she may still be looking for a causal or scientific answer to her question.

Put yourself in the child's place. Suppose something perplexes you. There was a fire in your building. You want an explanation. You may think in terms of holding some human being accountable—an arsonist, for example, or someone in the building who fell asleep while smoking. Or you may just be looking for a physical cause—such as a short circuit in the wiring. But whether you discover that the fire was intentionally set, or began unintentionally, is of less concern to you than that you want your mind to be put at rest as to how it happened.

So with children. They want to know how things happen. So they ask why. Don't assume that they're looking either for scientific—or for non-scientific explanations; they may have no idea of the difference. They're simply looking for explanations to put their mind at ease.

What they can do without is teasing—unless you can somehow convey to them that you're joking. If a child asks why you have a nose,

16

and you answer, "To hold my glasses up," the child may squeal with laughter. But the question is still unanswered.

Or, when the child asks. "Why does the moon follow us as we drive along the road?," you may think it appropriate to answer, "Because it likes us," or some such effort at humor. But you've merely avoided having to deal with a question you can't answer; you haven't satisfied the child's curiosity at all.

b. *Symbolic Interpretation*

Children, then, are often curious about the world, and their curiosity is partially satisfied by factual information and by explanations that provide them with causes or purposes of things.

But children sometimes want more. They want symbolic interpretations as well as literal ones. For these they turn to fantasy and play, to fairy tales and folklore—to the countless levels of artistic invention.

Children's folklore is a subculture all its own. Generation after generation of children pass through that culture, acquire a taste of its saucy doggerel, then pass on, forgetting it almost completely as they enter adolescence or maturity.

Have you forgotten the limericks you knew as a child, the gaily naughty jokes and riddles, the mad nonsense verse? Perhaps you've forgotten:

> Ladies and gentlemen,
> Take my advice,
> Pull down your pants,
> And slide on the ice.

but your students will acknowledge knowing it, if you ask them, although they'll be surprised you should want to know about such a trifle.

Children's folklore is sometimes ribald, and often zany, but one thing it's not: it's not children's literature written for children by adults. It comes from children themselves. It's an indigenous comic vision—although the sheer wackiness of much of it is laced with a grim echo of black or gallows humor.

The Opies have shown in detail the richness of children's folklore, and Erikson has amply shown how children's play and children's games can be understood as their efforts to come to terms with their experience.

On the other hand, children's literature is generally written *for* children rather than *by* children. And the chef d'oeuvre of the world of children's literature is the fairy tale.

The themes of fairy tales are so basic to human fantasy (whether children's or adults') that their origins are lost in the origins of

17

civilization itself. The love of the beautiful girl turns the beast back into a handsome prince, as the kiss of the handsome prince turns the sleeping beauty into a wide-awake one. Either we're beautiful but convinced at heart we're toads, or we're toads but at heart convinced we're beautiful. The themes are countless, and each is infinitely rich in the possibilities it spreads out for interpretation.

The point to note, however, is that the authors of fairy tales are grownups, and every grown-up is a potential spinner of such tales. "Tell me a story," children beg, and who can resist obliging when confronted with such pleading?

In doing so, however, one should know what one is doing. The fairy tale is captivating and beguiling. It fascinates its listeners, and casts a spell over them, from those very first words, "Once upon a time ..." The parent who invents stories for children nevertheless runs the risk of so indulging his own imagination as to pre-empt the child's imagination. We find delight in the creativity with which we express ourselves in such stories (and in the illustrations that go with them). But to what extent do we rob children of *their* creativity by doing their imagining for them?

If adults *must* write for children, then they should do so only to the extent necessary to liberate the literary and illustrative powers of those children. For example, we have resisted putting illustrations in the children's books we publish because we feel that to do so is to do for children what they should do for themselves: provide the imagery that accompanies reading and interpretation.

It remains a fact, of course, that our children's books are also adult-authored. Our excuse is first, that there is nothing wrong with adult stimulation of the powers of children—but such stimulation should be encouraging rather than overwhelming. We feel that our children's books encourage children's imagination rather then pre-empt it.

Second, our purpose is not to establish an immortal children's literature, but to get children thinking. If this purpose is attained, the instrument can self-destruct, as a match burns up once it has lit the fire. If our approach is correct, the fairy tale written by professional authors and the textbook written by professional scholars may eventually give way to children's books written by teachers and children themselves, yet incorporating the imagination and insight and understanding which such children acquire at each stage of their development.

What is important is that the imagination be de-professionalized: that children be encouraged to think and create for themselves, rather than that the adult world continue always to think and create for children. There is something unwholesome, even parasitical, in the thought of adults seeking to hold on to their own creativity by pre-empting the creativity of their own children.

But until we can devise effective ways of getting children to think for themselves, the least we can do is write books for them that will promote their creativity rather than diminish it.

c. *Philosophical Investigation*

Finally, children look for meanings that are neither literal (like scientific explanations) nor symbolic (like fairy tales), but which can only be called philosophical.

There are a great many types of questions which your children can ask you that can be called philosophical questions demanding philosophical answers. Obviously it isn't going to be easy for you to answer such questions, just as it wouldn't be easy for you to answer their arithmetical questions if you'd had no arithmetic.

Those philosophical questions which children most often raise are likely to be either *metaphysical, logical,* or *moral.* Let's look at some briefly.

(1) *Metaphysical* questions are very large questions, and most difficult to come to grips with. Metaphysics is philosophy at its most comprehensive. It involves issues of maximum generality.

You may wonder that your small children can raise such big issues. Yes, it is wonderful that they do. But equally remarkable is the fact that you probably used to do so yourself at one time, and have virtually forgotten how.

For example, suppose you ask your child what time it is. It's a simple question, and you hope you'll get a simple answer. Instead you find yourself under interrogation. "What's time?" the child asks. It's really quite stunning, when you come to think of it. "What's time?" How does one answer? Refer the child to St. Augustine, or Einstein? Read St. Augustine or Einstein oneself? The options look quite unpromising. So you say, "I didn't ask you what time was, I asked you what *the* time was." There, now—that should hold the little creature! For the moment, you've escaped. But you're beginning to recognize how formidable a child can be.

Or suppose you ask your children what the distance is between your home and the grocery store at which you shop. Since you've asked a very specific question, you expect a very specific answer—such as "a quarter-mile," or "six blocks." But to your surprise, they ask you "What's distance?" Not a particular distance, mind you, but distance in general. Now there you have a philosophical question; to be exact, a metaphysical question.

This manner of upstaging the normal level of dialogue by leaping to a more general level is typical of metaphysics. Instances of other metaphysical questions your children may already have posed you (or are quietly preparing for you) are these:

19

What's space?
What's number?
What's matter?
What's mind?
What are possibilities?
What's reality?
What are things?
What's my identity?
What are relationships?
Did everything have a beginning?
What's death?
What's life?
What's meaning?
What's value?

What makes questions like these particularly difficult to answer is that they involve such broad concepts that we can't find classifications to put them in—we just can't get a handle on them.

Normally, when we define terms, we do so by finding some broader context to which the given term belongs. For example, suppose you're asked by your children to define "man." Well, you might say that man's an *animal*. But if they keep after you, and insist on knowing what *kind* of animal man is, you might answer by saying that man's the animal that thinks. (Or you might answer by saying that man's the animal that laughs and cries, or any of a number of possible answers.)

But obviously, when your students ask you, "What's space?" you're going to have a pretty hard time trying to figure out a larger context in which space can be put. The same with words like "time" and "number." So questions like these are apt to be quite perplexing.

You may say, "Well, now, just because my students ask questions I don't know how to answer, that doesn't make them philosophers, does it? Surely they don't know they're asking metaphysical questions!"

They may not know it, but that's not the point. What's to the point is that children, with their need for wholeness and comprehensiveness, together with their naivete and lack of information, have a way of reaching out for total answers. It's all or nothing with them; not just how did this or that begin, but how did everything begin? Not just what is warm or cold, but what is temperature? Not just what is better or worse, but what is it for something to be perfect?

For example, this conversation about *perfection* was recently reported from a sixth-grade classroom:

Teacher: How would it be if, as Tony says here, everything were as clear and simple as it is in arithmetic?

1st student: It'd be perfect!

2nd student: But if it were perfect, nothing would need to be done!

3rd student: It'd be dull if there weren't anything to do!

4th student: Yes, and besides, if everything were perfect, you'd have perfect fools, and perfect messes ...

How quickly they got to the point of asking just what *perfection* might actually be like!

(2) *Logical* questions generally have to do with reasoning. In *Harry Stottlemeier's Discovery,* the children usually raise logical questions whenever they ask, "So what?" or "So what follows from that?" or "What can we figure out based on what we already know?"

For example, you're using logic when, having read a sign that says, "Closed Sundays," you figure out that the place is open Mondays through Saturdays.

You're using logic when you see that "spaniels bark" follows from the sentences "dogs bark" and "spaniels are dogs."

The relationship of logic to thinking is somewhat like the relationship of grammar to language. Grammar sets out the rules to conform to if we want to speak well. Logic sets up the standards that apply if we want to reason well.

One of the standards logic is concerned about is *consistency.* If your students mention to you that they did their homework, and then say a little later they they haven't yet done it, surely they would seem to be speaking inconsistently! What logic can do is emphasize the importance of consistency in our thinking, speaking, and acting.

(3) *Ethical Questions*

"What's good?" children want to know. "What's right?" "What's fair?"

Maybe they don't ask you. Maybe they don't even ask these questions ordinarily of one another. But they ask such questions of themselves. And if you get into a philosophical discussion with your students, you'll find out soon enough that they're concerned about morality, just as most people are.

They want to know what matters and what doesn't matter. They want to know what things are of importance—and therefore worth pursuing—and what things aren't.

Generally, when they want to know what's right to do, they don't even bother to ask you: they just observe what you do, and do likewise.

For example, suppose you frequently stress to them the importance of honesty, and they also observe that you respect other people's property. What will they learn from you?

Not just two things, but three. They will learn to advocate honesty, just like you. They will learn to respect other's property—just like you.

21

And they will learn how to keep their actions consistent with their pronouncements—just like you.

But now suppose that you take them on a class trip and upon packing to leave the hotel, they notice you stuffing hotel towels and ash trays into your luggage. What will they now learn from you?

Well, once again, three things, They will continue to advocate honesty—just like you. Also, they'll fail to practice it—just like you. And they'll come to believe that there should be inconsistency between what one preaches and what one practices.

So an understanding of consistency is important if children are to learn moral integrity. But the consistency has to be *practiced* by those whom the children take as their models of correct conduct—it won't be effective if it's merely *advocated* to them, or taught to them.

Nevertheless, it is logic which can best explain to us the nature of consistency: what it is for thoughts to be consistent with other thoughts; what it is for thoughts to be consistent with actions; and what it is for actions to be consistent with other actions. Training in logic can develop in children an *appreciation* for the consistency which is a basic condition of moral integrity. And training in logic can also develop in children an awareness of sound reasoning, such that, should departures from consistency be called for, children will recognize that they should have good reasons for making such departures.

Chapter Three

PHILOSOPHY

IN THE

CURRICULUM

1. THE GREEK EXPERIENCE

For the greater part of their history in Western civilization, literature and philosophy have been estranged from one another. But this was hardly the case during those early centuries in Greece which saw the emergence of philosophical thinking. Prior to Aristotle, in fact, philosophy was virtually always embodied in some literary vehicle. There were the aphorisms of Heraclitus and the poetry of Parmenides, just as there were later to be the dramatic dialogues of Plato.

Moreover there were literary events taking place in Greece which, while not themselves philosophical, had much to do with the philosophical consciousness and reflection that characterized Greek culture. One thinks here of the work of Homer, or of the dramatists of the 5th century, for these most certainly laid the groundwork for the systematic philosophical thought that followed.

But Homer was certainly no philosopher. How can he be credited with a major contribution to philosophical consciousness?

Let us recall that the *Iliad* is about the end of a war that presumably had occurred some three centuries before Homer's own day. We think of it as a war between the Greeks and the Trojans, but that is not quite correct. Before the war, there were only individual city-states on the peninsula that was to be called Greece. It was the war which made the inhabitants of those city states think of themselves as Greeks, just as it was the American Revolution which caused the colonists of the 13 states to think of themselves as Americans.

Our own American Revolution is only two hundred years behind us, but we still have strong feelings about it. We think of it as a "war for independence," and many Americans shake their heads incredulously upon learning that the British still refer to the event as the "rebellion of the Colonies."

In other words, we're still passionately partisan about that war, and so, evidently, are the British. Yet we consider ourselves sophisticated and highly civilized—especially when we contrast ourselves with the Greeks of the 12th century B.C., still a tribal people, hardly out of barbarism. The Greeks of Homer's day, a few centuries later, were presumably not much more civilized. They too must have looked back upon the war with Troy as the major unifying experience in their national history. So crude and fierce a people, we are inclined to think, would be no less hostile to a disparaging depiction of their ancestors than we would be today upon hearing unkindly references to our own forebears.

So we are surprised when we read the *Iliad* for the first time, and discover Homer's even-handed treatment of Greeks and Trojans alike. Here are heroic Trojans and cowardly Greeks; here too, brave Greeks and treacherous Trojans. Each side loses at least as much as it wins. Amidst all the petulance, stupidity, cunning and ferocity, only one individual stands out as noble—but he is not Greek, and his end is anything but a happy one.

One would think that the Greek people of Homer's day would have persecuted him for such an unflattering portrait of their patriotic heroes, but one is surprised to learn that the Greek populace apparently embraced the *Iliad* joyously. What manner of people could these have been?

Homer was no philosopher—but he treated the war impartially and objectively and detachedly. He admired what he thought admirable, whether it was Greek or Trojan. He depicted people as he saw them, regardless of nationality. It was a depiction that could have appealed only to a people that wanted to be told the truth about itself, regardless how much it hurt, just as the chief protagonist of *Oedipus* was later to demand to know the truth at all costs.

The impartial, objective pursuit of truth that the Greeks apparently recognized in Homer must have molded their own consciousness and must have whetted their appetite for a still greater independence of thought, so that the beginnings of philosophy in the 6th century were not greeted with persecution, although this occurred occasionally. The pre-Socratic "nature philosophers" of the 6th century may be scientific in their inspiration, but they are aphoristic and at times poetic in their manner of expression. Thus, when philosophy does finally make its appearance, it is at once philosophic in its originality and autonomy, scientific in its concern to propose statements as to the nature of things, and artistic in its mode of presentation.

Moreover, it was simple and popularly accessible, rather than technical or esoteric. Early philosophy was not for specialists, nor for a technical elite or a monastic minority. The aphorisms of the 6th century were rich and multi-leveled—yet anyone could understand them at some level.

But each philosopher issued his own pronouncements as though he alone existed, and philosophy needed a more dialectical tension. Once again, it was literature and drama which first provided what was needed. Thanks to Aeschylus, Sophocles and Euripides, philosophers were able to learn how to organize ideas dramatically; how to put them into sparkling interaction. And no one learned this lesson better than Plato.

But Plato also learns from Socrates—and learns, among many other things—that if the life of philosophy is dialogue, then the life of the philosopher is that of a teacher-learner—that philosophy is teaching as much as it is learning.

Ever since Plato, efforts to present philosophy in a manner that is popularly accessible and yet has authenticity and integrity have been few and far between. Nevertheless, we must take the Greek experience seriously and apply its lesson to the problem of our own age. For we too are in a society that is philosophically deprived—long on knowledge but short on wisdom. Philosophy comes to too few people, and even to those, it often comes too late.

But philosophy cannot be force-fed to people; they must want it. And they must somehow be motivated to want it—perhaps by the sorts of literary devices the Greeks employed. For the secret of the Greeks was not some special genius that was bestowed by nature on Athenian infants of the 5th century; it was more likely the happy legacy of Homer, whose fairness gave the Greeks a glimpse of justice, whose even-handedness gave them a glimpse of objectivity, and whose honesty gave them a glimpse of truth. A people that wants its posterity to be wise can do no better than create a vast repertory of artistic activities embodying those values whose pursuit it wishes to inculcate, much as the *Iliad* embodies the values prized by later generations of Greeks. Of foremost importance in that repertory will necessarily be a variety of new curricula that will help children think for themselves—

curricula that will provoke children to make and say and do more imaginatively and more thoughtfully than any of our curricula have done in the past.

2. THE USE OF THE PHILOSOPHICAL NOVEL IN THE PHILOSOPHY FOR CHILDREN PROGRAM

If education is supposed to begin with the student's experience (and since we have little knowledge of the experiential fund which any particular child brings into the classroom), we have little alternative than to create—or help the child create—the experience which is to be the start of the learning process. And the most efficient way to do this is by organizing material in such a fashion that, like a work of art, it produces experiences upon impact. Each such experience would contain the germs of the subject-matter to be introduced to children, but would also attempt to enlist their funded experience and imagination. In this way the children's academic present becomes relevant to their past and their future at once.

To the extent to which education is a preparation for further experience, it must acquaint the child with the fact that the world is full of complexity. Nothing can do this better than the fictional form. We do children a disservice if we equip them to approach the moral as well as other dimensions of life in an oversimplified manner. The novel as such affords an opportunity to sensitize the child to the ambiguities of life experiences and to the nuances and subtleties and ramifications of interpersonal behavior.

Philosophy in the literary vehicle of the aphorism or the poem begins with the pre-Socratics; philosophy as an art of dialogue may have begun with Socrates himself. But philosophy as a subject for study had to await the *Dialogues* of Plato. In the area of philosophy for children, it can likewise be said that it begins as an educational subject only when it develops a special genre of literature of its own: the philosophical children's novel.

If one looks at the great portraits of civilized conversation, ranging from Euripides to *Emma* and *Portrait of a Lady,* speech and thought are so wedded that the reader participates in the ebb and flow of ideas simultaneously with the ebb and flow of feeling. In the greatest portraits of the discovery of understanding, young men are shown together with old Socrates (or young Socrates with old Parmenides) exploring problems together. Socrates is portrayed as neither beautiful, in any conventional sense, nor again, in any conventional sense, is he shown to be wise, or as a dispenser or purveyor of wisdom.

The children's philosophical novel is an attempt to replace the traditional didactic text with a literary text that would be intrinsically

26

enjoyable, meaningful and valuable to the child. The student would enter into a community of children exploring problems that are important to them and in a way that has relevance to their own lives. At its best, the novel's beauty would be informative and its philosophical content would be organized and presented in such a way as to be a delight to the student.

The philosophy for children program consists of sets of materials designed for specific grade use. Each set is composed of a children's novel and an accompanying instructional manual. (Eventually, there will be a complete K-12 program: a set for K-2, 3-4; 5-6, 7-8; 9-10; 11-12. At the 9-10 level there will be four philosophical novels with accompanying manuals — one dealing with aesthetics, one dealing with philosophy of science, and one dealing with social philosophy and one dealing with the philosophical aspects of literature and language.)

The novels for grades 5-8 focus on formal and nonformal logic and their relation to metaphysical, aesthetic, epistemological and ethical issues. The novel for grades 5-6, *Harry Stottlemeier's Discovery,* is a story dealing with children who are roughly eleven or twelve years of age, and who are beginning to be interested in their thought processes. The book consists of seventeen chapters, in some of which children are found discovering some of the more general principles of human reasoning and inference, and in some of which they apply their discoveries to conversations about education, what is 'right' and 'wrong', the origin of the world, the nature of the mind, children's rights, differences between reasons and causes, the child's obligation to adult authority, treating people as things rather than as human beings, and so on. Adults play a relatively small role in the book, and the vocabulary, by and large, is at the 4th grade level. Philosophical terms and distinctions are virtually never used, and nowhere in the book do the children ever come to realize that they are engaged in philosophy.

Lisa, which is appropriate for the 7th and/or 8th grade, is a sequel to *Harry Stottlemeier's Discovery.* In this work the formal logic which was begun in *Harry* is completed, but again, embedded in a story which revolves around the daily experiences of the same children a year later. *Lisa* tends to focus on ethical and social issues which concern children at this time: lying and truth-telling, what is fair, what is right, what are rules, what are standards, what is natural. Issues such as job discrimination, sex discrimination, punishment, the nature of death, and the rights of children are also explored by the children in the novel. Throughout there is an increasing awareness of personal identity as well as of the complexity of interpersonal relationships.

The novel as a philosophy text affords the students in the classroom

27

an *indirect* mode of communication which, in a sense, safeguards the freedom of the child. Children are less inhibited when they feel that they are not the focus of the classroom attention. With the *distance* that the fictional technique obliges, they are left free to interpret and perhaps decide for themselves which philosophical views make the most sense to them, without the dread that they will come up with the morally 'wrong' answer, or that the discussion is part of a manipulative psychological diagnosis. When children find themselves reading about other children in a work of fiction, they tend to feel more at ease in discussing the affective aspects of the narrated life experiences; also, these affective aspects are integrated with the cognitive searchings of the fictional characters for ways of reasoning that will help them make sense of their experience. As these ways of reasoning are mastered, your students will begin to feel more in control and more self-confident. As the classroom dialogue ensues, this growing student self-confidence can become the foundation of an atmosphere of trust and openness wherein your students will feel free to discuss some of the philosophical concepts in relation to their personal lives.

The philosophical novel can also serve other purposes. It can act as a model of meaningful dialogue for your students. It can also act as a springboard for discovery processes about the laws of reasoning and their relation to issues that are important in children's lives. It can enable children to learn the difference between logical and illogical thinking. It can also indicate to them the occasions on which logical thought is appropriate and those on which non-logical thought might be preferable. Equally important, it is an excellent medium for sensitizing children to the complexity and frequent ambiguity of moral situations, and to the role of reasoning in such situations. Further, it can facilitate discussion, which can help bring about a deeper understanding among peers and between peers and adults, thus enhancing the social development of all who engage in such discussion. (There is detectable, in the novels, a development of adult character as well as of the character of children, as a result of their joint explorations of problems of mutual concern.)

3. THE FUNCTION OF THE INSTRUCTIONAL MANUAL

If the novel-qua-text is used, it is evident that the philosophical material that it contains can be presented only in broad brushstrokes. Thus, teachers need something in addition to help them explore the material in greater depth, so as to obtain a more comprehensive understanding of the concepts to be transmitted to the students. Moreover, suitable explanations are necessary to help the teacher relate such philosophical concepts to the student's in-school and out-of-school experiences. The instructional manual, therefore, must be a device for establishing connections between philosophy and the student's experience, as well as between philosophy and other school subjects that the students study. It must also contain strategies to help the teacher show students how to connect what they are studying in the present to their remembered past and imaginable future.

The instructional manual attempts to identify the leading philosophical ideas in each of the novels, and to provide a gloss on each of these concepts for the teacher. In a sense, it provides an explanation of the novel on many different levels.

Teachers should *not* use the commentary to organize their classroom discussions or to structure their 'lesson plan'. On the contrary, the discussion should always begin with what the students see and understand, and slowly move from a student-teacher dialogue to a student-student dialogue, in which children discuss ideas with each other, and build on each other's ideas. However, if the children in the classroom do not bring up some of the ideas embedded in the chapter, the teacher can use the manual commentary as a rich repertoire or fund from which to draw in order to explicate the content of the chapter at appropriate times.

Philosophical ideas can be easily forgotten unless they are reinforced. The instructional manuals are designed to introduce ideas early in the course, and to reintroduce them again and again, each time developing the concept in a more sophisticated fashion. You should try not to miss opportunities in the daily experiences of the classroom which demonstrate or throw light upon those concepts which have been introduced, so as to help the children recognize the multi-faceted ways in which philosophical ideas can relate to their lives.

Another way in which the instructional manuals aid the teacher in reinforcing the philosophical concepts is by providing a series of activities and exercises at the end of each chapter in which the concepts are related to *each* of the various subjects that the students study during the day. Thus there are exercises relating philosophical concepts to science, to social studies, to art, to mathematics, to language arts, to drama, to music, as well as additional exercises and activities designed solely to give children practice in dealing with metaphysical, ethical, epistemological and aesthetic issues which arise in their lives.

But remember: the objective of the educational process-or at least of its opening stages-is not to present a subject matter to the child, but to get the child to think in terms of that subject matter. Children should not have history thrust upon them as something alien and forbidding; rather, they must be induced to internalize it, so as to begin to think historically. Likewise, they should not be "given" drama, but should be induced to experience dramatically. They should not be presented with pictures to appreciate, unless doing so induces them to experience pictorially. The aim of the mathematics teacher is not merely to get children to memorize a number of rules and techniques, but to get them to think mathematically, as the aim of the logic teacher is to get children to think logically. And so, even though there is a vast body of learning which goes by the name of "philosophy," the point of philosophy for children is not to drum that body of knowledge into children's heads, but to keep them from abandoning their natural bent in the direction of thoughtfulness and speculation. The aim is not to get children to learn philosophy, but to encourage them to think philosophically.

Chapter Four

AIMS AND OBJECTIVES

OF THE

PHILOSOPHY FOR

CHILDREN PROGRAM

The main purpose of a program in philosophy for children is to help children learn how to think for themselves. But how does one accomplish this? What specifically can be accomplished by offering children a course in philosophical thinking?

1. IMPROVEMENT OF REASONING ABILITY

a. *The Origins of Reasoning*

Reasoning is too vast a topic to be discussed in a few paragraphs, and the cultivation of reasoning presents almost as many problems as reasoning itself.

In a sense, reasoning tries to do for the mind what medicine does for the body: both are remedial arts, trying to heal the frailties or injuries that mind or body are subject to. Think of the thousands of years which are spanned by the history of medicine. How much of that time was spent — and is still spent — in searching for specific remedies to specific ills! Here a tribe (or a "medicine man") finds an antidote to a poisonous substance; somewhere else another tribe devises potions intended to ward off disease. The aggregation of these preventive and curative stratagems, as thousands and hundreds of thousands of years are piled one upon the other, is simply overwhelming. The desperate, on-the-spot ways of curing become tributaries to medical understanding, and eventually the broad mainstream of medicine as a systematic discipline emerges.

But the savage must have recognized that there were errors of reasoning just as surely as there were bodily ills. Had he not thought so, and had he not thought both were corrigible, how could we ever have moved beyond savagery? But the way is tricky. The savage may have reached a point where he recognized that the proper approach for solving a problem is to treat the cause rather than the effect. He may also have reached a point where he realized that dirt breeds infection and that cleanliness is necessary for healing. And now he has an opportunity to put these two great realizations together. Here is a wound, and here is the knife that caused it. So he industriously scrubs and cleans the knife rather than the wound.

The path to rationality is not an easy one. Errors such as the one just recited are made by supposedly civilized people every day, as well as by savages. What is important however is the effort to correct, the struggle to rectify, the impulse to improve. Primitive man must have slowly become aware of the difference between better and worse reasoning, as he became aware of, say, the difference between harmless and poisonous mushrooms. We are not speaking here of the invention of formal logic, which is only a few thousand years old. We are speaking of the slow, painful growth of awareness that there are certain pitfalls which one must beware of in listening to others, just as there are pitfalls dug by hunters which other hunters must beware of. Indeed, the stratagems of early man must not have been limited to trapping game, but must have been devised to outwit one's fellow men as well, and such wily maneuvers must have invited counter-stratagems. We are referring then to that particular form of folklore known as nonformal logic, which may well have begun in early man's primitive efforts to weed out unproductive forms of thinking, and rid himself of the forms of thought he associated with unsuccess.

It is unlikely that reasoning is limited to humans. What seems more plausible is that humans discovered their own capacities to discover, explore and infer. That they invented tools was perhaps less important than that they discovered that they had the *capacity* to invent tools and all sorts of other things. That they invented language was perhaps less significant than that they employed it to analyze, to discuss, to reflect, and to speculate — all of which then expanded and

32

reinforced the languages they had invented.

Thus part of what we call reasoning consists of homely warnings descended from ancient times concerning the danger of accepting advice from people who are not authorities on the subject, or concerning the gullibility of those who are easily flattered, or concerning the mistake of thinking that if one event precedes another, the first must inevitably be the cause of the second. What we today call civilization very likely could not have occurred had there not been primitive men who cared about the hygiene of dialogue, and who could assert "Just because you're a good fisherman, it doesn't mean you know anything about hunting wild boar," or "Just because you say an incantation every evening, it doesn't mean you make the stars come out at night," or even, "Flattery won't help you persuade me."

The sum of this kind of lore is what we have been speaking of as nonformal logic. It embodies our suspicions of certain forms of reasoning as being unsound, and to be avoided. It consists less of recommendations for correct reasonings than of prohibitions against incorrect reasonings. It identifies fallacies as the reefs and sandbars upon which the ship of reason can all too easily run aground — but it is as yet a ship with neither mast nor rudder. These appear only with the beginnings of philosophy.

We are naturally more struck by the lurid and colorful aspects of life than by the prosaic, and there is no doubt that the drama of good versus evil, the clash of moral values, strikes us much more forcefully than the dry bones of logic. We prick up our ears at "Thou shalt not lie," forgetting that the broad human context of such an injunction has to do with the need for consistency in human discourse. The rough lessons of experience must have provided evolving man with wisdom enough to see that inconsistencies are trouble-makers. One must get one's story straight — i.e., consistent with the facts, and the parts of it consistent with one another. Moralists may denounce lying as immoral, but folklore sees it as inexpedient. From the point of view of practical sagacity, the counsel not to lie is like the counsel not to contradict oneself, except that the self-contradiction is more flagrantly disadvantageous. There is, of course, considerably more to morality than the logical aspect we have been pointing to. There are components of self-respect and respect for others which have not been alluded to at all. But the point is that these latter components, though valid enough, are not so easily demonstrated to children as the need to avoid self-contradiction and the need for consistency. Mutual respect can best be taught children by encouraging them to engage in activities in which they discover its merits, rather than by explaining it to them or by exhorting them to it. But consistency can be both practiced *and* explained. There is thus a distinct advantage to stressing in elementary education the logical underpinnings of morality.

Naturally there are objections that can be cited with regard to the above approach. It seems to appeal to expediency and to the child's selfish interests, rather than to character, conscience and duty. But exhortations to duty and conscience appear to be increasingly less promising as sources of moral dispositions. If moral character is to be constructed, it will have to employ the child's interests as its means and materials.

Consistency is only one of the features stressed by a philosophically oriented education. It is of equal generality and importance to help the child see connections and make distinctions. We help children perceive connections when we give them practice in grouping and classifying, and show them how their everyday behavior presupposes the ability to make such classifications. We help them make distinctions when we encourage them to say both *what* doesn't belong to a given group or class, and *why* it doesn't.

Connections can also be thought of as relationships, and along with instance-kind class relations, there are two other major families of outstanding importance in education, requiring particular attention from the teacher. The first consists of cause-consequence connections; the second consists of part-whole connections. It is unfortunate that our emphasis upon science has led us largely to ignore the second of these types, while giving the bulk of our attention to the first. Our notion of intelligence is all too often addressed only to matters of practical control over practical affairs, and understanding of cause-consequence connections seems most appropriate to such control. But intelligence is no less a matter of perceiving what the parts of a situation are, how they relate to one another, and to the whole to which they all belong; it is also a matter of understanding how to *construct* wholes out of materials that then come to serve as parts. Every art class in the school is a laboratory for such intelligence, and if education has as one of its goals the enlargement of intelligence, then the stress on the understanding of part-whole relationships should be emphasized no less than the understanding of the relationship of causes and consequences. It is because philosophy treats both forms of intelligence as valid and important (unlike science, which stresses only the one, or art, which stresses the other), that it is so eminently *valuable as a methodology of educational practice.*

b. *Reasoning in Childhood*

Wondering at what age an infant begins to reason is a bit like wondering at what age an embryo becomes a person. Both questions presuppose that a particular age can be specified at which these monumental changes occur, and we know so little about the pre-natal and the early post-natal life of the child, and that it is extremely difficult to specify the origins of infantile reasoning.

We can say that reasoning begins with inference, but it is no simple matter to distinguish the early stages of inferential behaviour from instinctual behavior. There is the anecdote, no doubt apocryphal, attributed to the ancient Roman writer Sextus Empiricus, that a dog can be said to draw an inference if, when following a scent, he comes to a fork in the road, and after sniffing the first two paths with negative results, proceeds down the third path *without sniffing*. But what of the infant who reaches for the breast of someone who picks him up? We attribute it to instinct, but why can it not be the conclusion of a practical syllogism: In the past, breasts have nourished me; This is a breast; Therefore it nourishes, where the action of reaching is tantamount to the conclusion? It is true that the child would not have had the facility with language to formulate the premises linguistically. But this is not necessary, so long as the child has acquired habits translatable into such premises. In other words, children can be said to think inductively and deductively long before they begin to use language. What language does is to symbolize such behavior and permit its formalization.

Likewise, a single counterinstance may be sufficient to alert an infant to the inapplicability of the habit which is the non-verbal counterpart of a generalization. Thus the infant may have developed a particular habitual response to a configuration of behavior which it identifies as its parent. This response is a trusting response, let us say. Now a traumatic event occurs. The parent carelessly puts the child in a bath which is too hot. Result: a substantial loss of trust by the infant in its parent. The generalization about the parent's trustworthiness no longer holds, so the infant infers that its own trusting response is no longer called for.

Obviously one could go on and on with examples of this kind, in which habitual rules are learned, then modified in the light of counterinstances. One could explore the rudiments of psychological associations, or the tendency of children to complete perceptual patterns, for all of these represent the manner in which the child moves from what is immediately given to what is not. Hence all of these represent the foundations of inference, which is to say they represent the foundations of reasoning.

But when, it may well be asked, does the child begin to reason *philosophically*? For although all philosophical activity involves reasoning, it does not follow that all who reason are engaged in philosophical activity. Children begin to think philosophically when they begin to ask why.

The word "why" is surely one of the small child's favorites. Yet its uses are anything but simple. There are two main functions which, it is generally agreed, are performed by the question "Why?" The first is to elicit a causal explanation, the second to determine a purpose.

To explain something causally is to allude to conditions which give rise to that thing or event. You explain the ice on the sidewalk by referring to the cold front that arrived during the rainstorm last night. You explain the burning of the factory by referring to the match that started it, or to the fact that the building had just been struck by lightning.

To ask to know the purpose is to ask what a thing is made for, or what an activity is done for. The purpose of the bridge is to convey traffic. The purpose of a pen is to serve as an instrument for writing. Weatherstripping is put around a door in order to conserve heating fuel.

Among questions to determine purposes, some ask for what purpose a person does something he chooses to do. Explanations which account for choices are called justifications, and are said to provide reasons rather than causes. If we ask why an arsonist set a fire, we are presumably asking for his reasons. The answer, however, could cite either a purpose or a cause. If the answer is that he is a pyromaniac and has an uncontrollable obsession, then we are being given a causal explanation of his behavior. But if the answer is that he set the fire on purpose, *in order to* collect the insurance, then the answer is in the form of a reason.

Children are interested in both purposes and causes, and they constantly blend these usages of the question "Why?", or seek to distinguish one from the other. Thus the child may ask why there was a hailstorm, and may appear to accept the meteorological explanation offered by a teacher about the causes of hailstorms. But the child may very well have been looking for a justification rather than an explanation. "For what behavior was the hailstorm sent as a punishment?" may have been the question he had in mind. On other occasions, of course, the reverse may happen. He wants a causal explanation for the disappearance of his drum, and instead we give him a justification.

We endeavor to help the child distinguish between justification and explanation when we try to teach him the difference between things done "on purpose" and things that are "just accidents." Children are taught that they are accountable for what was done deliberately, but not for what happens accidentally. Accidents can be explained, and one need not justify one's conduct if one has been involved in a genuine accident. On the other hand, children learn, one can be punished for deliberately doing what one had been warned not to do, for doing such things on purpose.

To the Stoic philosophers of ancient times, this distinction was of major importance — knowing the difference between what lies within one's power to do, and what does not. For one can feel totally absolved of responsibility for what happens outside one's power. The child's "why?" can be seen as a similar effort to identify what should be accounted for by reasons, and to distinguish this from the realm of causal explanations.

The child asks "why?" very early in childhood, and so can very early be considered to be engaged in philosophical behavior. Indeed, the young child is so persistent at this that, in comparison with the lack of curiosity characteristic of adults, we are tempted to speak of the individual's philosophical behavior as declining with increase of age. This contrasts sharply with the child's increase of information and facility in the use of conceptual instruments.

No doubt the child's capacity to perform certain tasks set for him by experimenters increases with age, from relatively simple arithmetical tasks to more complex ones, and still more complicated ones. Since experimenters tend to assume that gradations of intelligence conform to gradations of ability to perform these tasks, they view growing up as a unilinear pilgrimage from incompetence to competence. Losses are nowhere taken into account. The decline of imagination, of one's sense of harmony with surroundings, of one's curiosity about the world, these are not considered losses at all, when maturity is equated with doing tasks considered to be the hallmarks of responsible adulthood.

Thus it is that normal children are said to mature through acquiring language, forgetting that the language would be useless did the infant not have dispositions to acquire and utilize it. Thus too children are said to acquire rationality, although the masses of information they acquire would be useless did they not have dispositions to process it so as to discover its relevance and meaning Only in the area of children's art is it admitted that children possess abilities — a power of organization and a feeling for form — which gradually disintegrate until they are in danger of being altogether lost. But when art is not taken seriously as an index of rationality, the decline of artistic power in the middle years of childhood is deemed irrelevant to the growth of intelligence, and in any event no great loss.

Since our culture characteristically defines intelligence in terms of the ability to answer questions rather than the ability to ask them, and in terms of competence in solving problems rather than competence in recognizing and formulating them, it is little wonder that philosophy and childhood are generally thought to be mutually exclusive. Philosophy has been traditionally conceived to be the preserve of the elderly. By a curious perversion of logic, we ignore authentic manifestations of philosophical reasoning in childhood, we virtually ignore children's need to be challenged and assisted to develop their philosophical powers, and then conclude that philosophy is inherently unsuitable for young people: that they have neither talent for it nor interest in it.

The intellectual progress typically credited to children occurs not when they learn to think for themselves, but when we note with satisfaction that the content of their thought has begun to approximate the content of our own — when their conceptions of the world begin to resemble ours. Until children view reality as adults do, the richness and preciousness of their views of the world are repeatedly disparaged and discouraged. This is particularly true of prevailing conceptions of "moral development," where certain notions such as universalizability are taken to represent the summit of moral thought. In other words, children whose moral views approximate those of the psychological researchers are assigned a higher level on the scale of moral development than those whose views differ from the moral outlook of the investigators.

The child who displays originality and independence of thought is likely to come to unpopular conclusions, and may very well arrive at some conclusions which are in fact quite wrong. It is easy enough to correct a wrong conclusion; it is quite something else to sustain originality, or to revive it in a child who has been led to suppress it.

Adults sensitive to philosophical implications and to philosophical originality are much more likely to nurture children's speculations and insights than adults lacking such experience and sensitivity. Not long ago, a Chicago mother, with some background in philosophy, reported that her four-year-old daughter, when told to turn off the water in the bathtub, had replied, "Don't worry, it won't run over, because from the water to the top of the tub, it just keeps getting less." No one familiar with the paradoxes of Zeno can fail to recognize here that offbeat way of looking at the world, such as is exemplified in the parable of Achilles and the Tortoise. (Trying to catch the tortoise, Achilles halves the distance between it and himself with every step, thus being assured of never overtaking it.) In this instance, the child's conclusion is *literally* wrong: the water *will* overflow the tub. But what thoughtful originality nonetheless! Such a remark as this little girl's, if listened to seriously, could be the point of departure for an exciting discussion of the ways and processes of nature (after turning off the water!).

Or take this comment reported by the father of a 7-year-old Parisian boy: "When we are dead, we dream that we are dead." Such a remark might well be dismissed by an adult with no interest in philosophy as being meaningless. Yet it would seem to represent an insight enormously rich in metaphysical implications, indicating that the

38

child may have a powerful speculative imagination. Children generally do not develop their intuitions systematically. But the teacher can encourage children to explore the implications of their original insights, so that the treasure of their perceptions and intuitions may not be lost.

Not long ago, in reviewing a videotape of a classroom dialogue, we picked up an interchange between two boys ten years of age, regarding personal identity. One boy remarked that it is our thoughts that make us the persons we are. The other replied, "No, because last night I dreamt I was dead, and yet here I am." Obviously this latter child has intimated, with this remark, a much more systematic notion than he has expressed. His comment begs for elaboration and interpretation: if he *is* his thoughts and he has thought (dreamed) he is dead, then he really must be dead. But here he is, alive, though he's dreamed he is dead. So he cannot just be his thoughts. There is use of an important logical pattern here, of stating a hypothesis (here as an If ... then --- statement), then denying the second part of it and thereby showing the first to be false.

As part of our own curriculum for grades 5 and 6, we present a discussion plan on children's rights which begins with the question "Did you ask to be born?" It is a question many children have themselves raised. In the context of classroom discussion, the question being thrown back at them, the children may at first treat it with ridicule. How indeed *could* someone not yet born ask to be born? Then other voices are heard, suggesting that perhaps the question is not quite as silly as it sounds, and that perhaps the issue of the child's consent should not be dismissed without serious discussion.

Estimations of childhood intelligence has often been the work of investigators whose approach to the problem is wholly observational and detached. Very often, we measure children's abilities to do things *we* want them to do, rather than assess their capacities to do what they themselves choose to do. We set them tasks and then measure their responses; yet these tasks can seem to them like chores to be avoided. Merely regarding what children do in response to adult demands is a poor substitute for evaluating what they can do when their own interests and their own problems come to the fore. The merit of philosophy for children is that it allows the classroom to become a forum for an airing of issues relevant to children's own problems, diverse enough so that the appeal is not just to the manipulative aspect of a child's intelligence, but to the contemplative and creative aspects as well. Adult intervention need not be aimed at bringing the child strictly into line with the adult perspective of reality, but rather at facilitating children's explorations of their own thoughts and experiences through the use of philosophical techniques derived from the inexhaustibly rich philosophical tradition.

c. *Reasoning and Inference*

One of the most serious difficulties experienced by elementary school children is in the area of the drawing of inferences. The child may have a problem with perceptual inferences, logical inferences or evidential inferences.

(1) *Perceptual Inferences.* Children may have 20-20 vision and yet have difficulty drawing inferences from what they see. They come home to a house where the doors are normally kept locked, find the door open, and it may still not occur to them that something is different. The child perceives adequately, but fails to draw the obvious perceptual inference. The child's hearing may be perfectly all right, he hears the car horn yet fails to infer that a car is coming at him. These difficulties are not limited to children: there are adults who likewise have trouble drawing basic inferences from what they see or hear or taste or smell.

(2) *Logical Inferences.* Another type of difficulty a child may experience has to do with the drawing of an inference from one or more *statements.* For example, if someone tells him that winters at the equator are never cold, the child should be able to infer that the statement, "Last winter was cold at the equator" is false. And a child should know that given the statement, "Some people are tall," it does *not* follow that "All people are tall."

(3) *Inferences From Evidence.* Sometimes a person is confronted by groups of facts of various sorts. For example, a child visits a foreign country, observes parades, children with flags and banners, speeches and singing, and concludes that "it must be some sort of national holiday." This is an inference drawn from observable evidence.

Children who experience difficulties with any or all of the above-mentioned types of inferences are likely to experience academic difficulties as well. The child may be able to read well, but doesn't interpret what has been read because of a difficulty with drawing inferences from the material. A child may do good work in a laboratory when given specific directions but then be at a loss when asked about the meaning of what was done: the child observes effects but has trouble inferring causes. Or the child may observe countless instances of the same kind but not infer that there may be a rule or a law involved.

Such children may be experiencing an "inference block," and this kind of block very likely *cannot* be resolved by repetitious exercises or memorization of rules of thinking. In fact, there is no easy solution to an "inference block." This course in philosophical thinking can perhaps contribute to an alleviation of the problem, by helping children to engage in processes of inferring by creating a milieu which encourages them to do so. Philosophy for children should encourage them to draw better inferences, help them to identify evidence, and assist them in recognizing inferences that are faulty. Much can be accomplished if children can be brought via their own experience to understand the feasibility of going beyond what they see and read, and developing the capability for drawing inferences. As long as they are stuck with the concrete perceptions and verbal expressions that surround them, they may feel so overwhelmed by it all that they cannot bring themselves to get up and over the content and facts, and begin the *process of thinking*. It is for this reason that teaching which emphasizes content to the exclusion of the *process* of inquiry is so damaging to children in the long run.

2. DEVELOPMENT OF CREATIVITY

It is an unfortunate part of traditional education that training in logical rigor is often assumed to take place only at the expense of imagination and creativity. As if, for the child's logical proficiency to be developed, spontaneity and imaginativeness would need to be suppressed. The approach taken in this program supposes on the contrary that logical thinking can be encouraged by means of creative activity, and conversely, that creativity can be fostered with the development of logical ability. The two go hand in hand.

In this program, we have endeavored to suggest various kinds of creative play activities: games, dramatizations, puppetry, and other art forms, all of which directly or indirectly contribute to children's ability to express their experience and to explore the consequences and meanings of such expressions.

Adults are too frequently prone to underestimate the heavy penalty which our society places upon the child's free imagination and creativity. The more insecure the child's life is, the more precarious the surroundings, the more of a luxury it is to engage in a rich fantasy life, imagining things as they might be, instead of confronting the grim reality of things as they are. The inner-city child, or for that matter, any child who must deal on a day-to-day basis with the perils of poverty, crime and other aspects of social disorganization, cannot easily shake off this atmosphere of concrete fact, so as to be able to enjoy the delights of fairy tales and the escapades of imaginary children and other imaginary creatures in imaginary environments.

In the past, we have treated the faulty inferences that have resulted from invalid thinking as just so much intellectual trash. We have failed to realize that under some circumstances it can actually be beneficial for the child to explore the results of invalid reasoning. This is not to deny that many situations call for nothing less than rigorous, logical thinking. But there are many others to which fantasy and make-believe are quite appropriate. For instance, logical fallacies can help encourage the child to consider counterfactual situations. It is logically invalid to deduce from the statement, "All onions are vegetables," that "All vegetables are onions." But, if children are encouraged to contemplate what a world would be like in which all vegetables were onions, they may very well delight in thus picturing to

41

themselves its details: one would cry when peeling carrots, smell onions every time one sliced potatoes, etc. Obviously, this does more than liberate the children's imagination; it frees their inventiveness as well.

Helping children grow means that, at every stage, challenges appropriate to that stage have to be devised. It is not enough to challenge them to develop their logical ability alone, although such development is certainly necessary. Their growth depends upon stimulating their inventiveness and creativity as well. Unless children can imaginatively envisage how things might be, and how they themselves might be, it will be difficult for them to set goals toward which they can grow.

3. PERSONAL AND INTER-PERSONAL GROWTH

It is as yet not precisely known what effects this course may have on the children's emotions, interests, attitudes or other aspects of their personal development. Pilot projects that have been conducted so far indicate a difference of spirit in the classroom which could very well be infectious and could translate itself into a heightened eagerness to learn and share with others, together with the development of other aspects of the individual personality. Much more investigation is needed, however, before it can be confidently asserted that the program can produce a significant increase in self-confidence, emotional maturity and a general self-understanding.

For most children, learning to think philosophically takes place primarily in the process of interpersonal discussion, and in the reflection that follows such a discussion. Children who merely read the philosophical novel, and are deprived of the opportunity to discuss their interpretations of it with their classmates and their teacher will be deprived of a wealth of meanings which the book is capable of suggesting, but which only a discussion can bring out. Most elementary school textbooks, it is true, are not thought of as vehicles for the promotion of interpersonal communication. But *Harry Stottlemeier's Discovery* and *Lisa* are children's books that are to be both read *and* discussed.

The discussion, in turn, brings other advantages. In particular, it promotes children's awareness of one another's personalities, interests, values, beliefs and biases. This increased *sensitivity* is one of the most valuable by-products of classroom communication. Unless children have some insight into the nature of the individuals with whom they share their lives, they are not likely to make sound judgments regarding them. It does no good to teach children social rules if they are so insensitive that they cannot detect when and how to use them. Unless interpersonal sensitivity is fostered and encouraged as a *prerequisite* for the child's social development, that social development will be thwarted. There can be little reason to expect sound social judgment from the child unless interpersonal insight is first cultivated, and such insight is often the product of successful philosophical dialogue.

However, if it should turn out that sensitivity and judgment are enhanced by the program, it may well be that the program has served not simply to accelerate children's growth, but to *enlarge their very capacity for* growth. The teacher can make an indispensable contribution to this process. Any living thing goes through a process of growth, but the enlargement of the capacity for growth is something that is likely to occur only under the influence of a caring, concerned and knowledgeable teacher. The capacity for growth will no more enlarge by itself than a ball will roll by itself up an inclined plane. Children must be treated in such a way that their *powers begin to reenforce each other,* rather than counteract each other. Under proper educational conditions, this process of reenforcement can generate in children a *mutually reenforcing set of intellectual and emotional activities* which can pull them well beyond where they would have been had these factors been developed in isolation from one another.

4. DEVELOPMENT OF ETHICAL UNDERSTANDING

There is a contemporary controversy about the relationship between morality and education. Members of opposing camps generally group themselves and each other in the following ways. There are those who contend that all education has a moral dimension. There are those who insist that under no circumstances should educators attempt to introduce morality into the classroom because it will inevitably, as they see it, be nothing more than indoctrination. Thirdly, there are those who maintain that a sound education can and should contain a component of moral education.

When problems of morality and education are thus formulated, we are not able to take a position among them. Each of these groups presupposes that morality consists of moral principles and rules; most of their disagreements can be traced to disagreements about which rules should be taught, or whether they should be taught at all. In our view, a philosophical approach to ethics is one which stresses the *method* of ethical inquiry rather than the particular moral rules of particular adults. The teacher of philosophy assumes that getting children to reason logically about matters to which logic applies will be genuinely helpful for the solution of human problems, including moral ones. The teacher of philosophy likewise believes that without awareness of the metaphysical, epistemological, aesthetic and other aspects of human experience, ethical inquiry alone will be myopic and unsound. Again, the teacher of philosophy will be concerned to encourage students to see the importance of arriving at sound moral judgments, and this requires the development in such students of ethical sensitivity, care and concern. Thus, as ethics is presented in the context of philosophy for children, it is concerned not to inculcate substantive moral rules, or alleged moral principles, but to acquaint the student with the *practice* of moral inquiry.

It should be evident that we stress helping children become aware of the nature of moral judgments, rather than pressuring them into making moral decisions or to "advance" to some "higher" stage of moral decision-making. From our point of view, judgment is only one aspect in the life of an ethical individual. Such judgment must be conditioned by moral awareness and moral intelligence. Moreover, the moral individual is not only one who is adept at making "right" judgments, but is equally one who knows when judgments are *not* called for and avoids making them in such situations.

Chapter Eight of this book is an extended discussion of the relationship of philosophy to moral education. Since the topic is enormous, even this chapter should be considered only as an introduction, but hopefully it will give some guidance in understanding the problems and dimensions of ethical education.

5. SPECIFIC PHILOSOPHICAL OBJECTIVES

Other goals of this course in philosophical thinking can be listed as a set of discoveries:

a. Discovering alternatives

b Discovering impartiality.

c. Discovering consistency.

d. Discovering the feasibility of giving reasons for beliefs.

e. Discovering comprehensiveness.

f. Discovering situations.

g. Discovering part-whole relationships.

a. *Discovering alternatives*

How do children learn to think of "fresh alternatives?" How do they learn that the way they now think is not the only way they *could* think?

One way they can do so is by developing the habit of always considering the possibility that the *negative* of their idea might be correct. The child who sees the sun rise and thinks that "the sun moves around the earth" learns to think that maybe "the sun doesn't move around the earth" — and this long before anyone actually tells him that it doesn't. The child who thinks that "the earth is flat," but is at the same time critically aware that the negative is possible, will also entertain the thought that "the earth is not flat." Every factual statement has a negative which could possibly be true.

Even more simple is taking the idea of something (not a statement but just the thought of some thing or activity) and finding its negative. The negative of "playing" is "not playing." The negative of "laughing" is "not laughing." We can even say that the negative of "chair" is "non-chair," or that the negative of "table" is "non-table."

The child who works with these notions will begin to see that when thoughts and their negatives are put into order, they begin to display a pattern of alternatives. For example, suppose the child thinks of "working," and when the negative is considered, the result is "not working." But "not working" may be interpreted by the child as "playing," so now there are two thoughts the child has, "working" and "playing." And now there are four alternatives:

(1) working and playing
(2) working but not playing
(3) playing but not working
(4) neither working nor playing

The child may now find that a similar set of four alternatives can be developed for any pair of ideas whatsoever: milk and fudge, or crocodiles and triangles, or icicles and dandelions.

Up to now the child may only have been vaguely aware of alternatives and not fully appreciative of them as possibilities. Chances are, if the child thinks of *sick* and *hungry,* he is only dimly aware of *sick but not hungry, hungry but not sick,* and *neither sick nor hungry.* So if you ask the child is there a lot of sickness and hunger in the world today, the child could well say yes. But if you ask about the other three *possibilities,* the child will likely shake its head. A world from which sickness and hunger have been virtually eliminated: *impossible!* Yet a simple demonstration in the child's own logic would show that something may be possible, even if it isn't practical or feasible or likely at this moment.

And this is what is meant by learning to discover fresh alternatives. It means considering all the possibilities. Nor do these other possibilities have to be as idealistic as in the previous example. A child who is aware that he is healthy and well-fed may never really have given much thought to what it would be like to be *well-fed but sick,* or *healthy but hungry,* or hungry and sick together. Or, if the child's family is planning a vacation trip, they may discuss whether to go by bus or train, and the child can point out that while they can go by either one, they might also go part way by each, or they may choose not to use either mode of transportation, and go in some different fashion, such as by plane. What is important is to give the child practice in examining situations for *alternative* solutions that might otherwise be overlooked.

b. *Discovering impartiality*

As adults, we certainly are aware that we are often *partial* rather than impartial. We enthusiastically root for the home team, and accuse the umpire or referee of being biased towards the other side. If an accident happens, we generally consider ourselves innocent and the other fellow guilty. In politics, it is often our candidate who can do no wrong, while his opponent is incapable of doing anything right.

Now, there is nothing wrong with such partiality in itself. Why shouldn't a mother be partial to her own child, or a lawyer to his client, or a girl to her boyfriend? Obviously, there are situations that will call for partiality, yet there are others in which partiality is very definitely wrong. We wouldn't want a judge who shows partiality; we find it difficult to condone the parent who favors one of his children over the others or who always makes one the scapegoat; and if someone agrees to mediate a quarrel — whether between individuals or between nations — it just won't do for that person to exhibit partiality.

So it's a question of knowing when to be partial and when to be impartial. The trouble is that partiality seems to come easily to most people, while they only learn impartiality the hard way.

Now there is one situation in which impartiality is particularly appropriate. It's the situation in which you're trying to understand something. You begin by trying to understand it solely in terms of your own point of view. You may pay little attention to how other people have experienced the matter. Let's say a friend tells you of a new regulation, and you get pretty worked up about it, because you're certain that it's a stupid rule. And all you want to do at first is tell everyone how you feel. But after you get the matter off your chest, you begin to listen to other people. Some may agree with you, and some may disagree. And you may begin to see that maybe your initial judgment of the new regulation was too hasty. Maybe it has certain merits you didn't at first recognize. Or maybe it's even worse than you first thought it to be. But in either case, you've learned from the other people's experience. You've learned to see things from their points of view as well as your own. You've begun respecting them for their opinions as much as you respect yourself for your own. And you've begun to rise above your own original, partial estimate of the situation so as to be a more objective and impartial judge of it.

It's just this experience of impartiality that we have got to make available to children. It is too much to expect them to be naturally

46

objective and impartial, although perhaps some of them are. But they can all learn to be, and they learn a lot more quickly if we encourage them by arranging situations in which they can try to talk objectively and impartially about *their* problems.

Discovery of the usefulness of impartiality can be illustrated by referring to a situation observed not long ago in a sixth-grade classroom.

Teacher:	Do Lisa and Fran have the same attitude towards Harry Stottlemeier?
A boy:	He bothers Lisa, but he doesn't bother Fran.
Teacher:	Why does he bother Lisa?
A girl:	Maybe he just doesn't like boys.
Teacher:	Why do you say that?
Girl:	I dunno. Maybe she thinks boys are always claiming to do better than girls, and she doesn't go along with that.
A boy:	Well, they *are* better than girls!
Girl:	No, they ain't, neither!
Teacher:	What do the rest of you think? Are boys better than girls? No, don't all answer at once! One at a time.
Boy:	Yeah, boys are better than girls.
Teacher:	Do you mean in everything, or just in some things?
Boy:	They're better than girls in sports.
Girl:	They're better than girls in *some* sports, maybe, but there are sports, like maybe volleyball, where we're better than they are.
Boy:	There are plenty of boys better than girls in girl's sports.
Girl:	Maybe a few of them are, but in *most* girls' sports, *most* girls are better than most boys.
Boy:	Okay, but in most *boys'* sports, most boys are better than most girls.

Teacher:	Are you saying that there are some girls who are better than most boys, even in boys' sports?
Boy:	Could be.
Girl:	So it isn't true, what you first said, that boys are better than girls!

The conversation moved along after this to other topics, but the point must have been obvious to everyone in the class. They had begun with very sweeping statements, both boys and girls making tremendous generalizations about "all boys" and "all girls." But gradually, they had to admit exceptions. And gradually each side began to take a more factual, more objective, more impartial attitude towards the relative strengths of girls and boys. They compared attitudes and opinions, they exchanged biases, but what emerged was a kind of consensus, with each child taking a more unbiased position than that with which he or she began.

c. *Discovering consistency*

It would be very silly, you'll no doubt agree, if someone were to say something like this:

> Goliath was very big
> Israel was not very big.

Therefore, Goliath was bigger than Israel.

The trouble with the above reasoning is obviously that Goliath was "big" compared with *people,* while Israel wasn't big when compared with other *countries.* So "big" means something different in each case, with the result that the conclusion is false. The person speaking has used the word "big" *inconsistently.*

Or suppose someone else was silly enough to say this:

> No man lives forever.
> But women aren't men.

Therefore, women live forever.

Once again, a word is being used *inconsistently.* First the word "men" is used to mean all human beings. Then it's used to mean just male human beings. So it's an invalid, illogical kind of reasoning, and the conclusion does not follow.

Now let's consider a different kind of inconsistency. Suppose someone makes a sweeping statement like, "Everything that goes up must come down." But then he adds, "Of course, we send rockets into outer space, and they don't come back down." He probably isn't aware that his second statement contradicts his first statement. And since his second statement is true, his first statement must be false. So once again we have the problem of a person who takes a position, and then doesn't stick to it. In effect, he too is guilty of *inconsistency*.

Cases such as those mentioned above represent careless thinking. When we realize we've been thinking in a sloppy sort of way (and inconsistency is usually an example of mental sloppiness), we may be amused by it, or we may be ashamed of it, or both. But children should no more be encouraged to be inconsistent in their reasoning than they should be encouraged to multiply or subtract incorrectly. Indeed, how would it be if some days, when one added, say, 4 and 5, one got 9, and on other days one got 17 or perhaps 3? Picture such a person looking after your bank account!

Children have to be encouraged to use their words carefully from a very early age. They should be made aware of how the meaning of words in a statement or paragraph can shift their meanings.

If people insist on being inconsistent, the least we can do is to ask them to explain their reasons for doing so. Maybe if they can't find reasons for being inconsistent, they'll come to think of the practice as indefensible, and will try being reasonable for a change.

Another example of inconsistency is the following, paraphrased from a news release by a noted educator:

"Although inflation has produced many serious problems in the area of higher education, there may be a silver lining to the cloud.As a result of the higher cost of education, many poorer students will not be able to go to college. But the colleges have been looking for some way to get rid of the poorer students anyhow. So maybe it will all work out for the best."

Obviously, there is a shift of meaning here from the first use of the word "poorer" meaning *economically* poorer and the second use of the word "poorer" meaning *academically* poorer. Doubtless, the person who made this statement didn't consciously intend to imply that colleges should be glad to get rid of students who were not financially well-off, but that's what can be inferred from his statement just the same.

Together with verbal inconsistencies, there are also inconsistencies of words and actions and of actions alone. When a teacher tells a child that she is deeply concerned with his welfare but then ignores him, or if a person holds a door for you but then at the last moment lets it go in your face, we see an inconsistency between words and actions or between actions which are at cross-purposes. These types of inconsistencies are related to the sorts of verbal inconsistencies previously mentioned. For example, they can be described by means of contradictions ("She was and was not concerned with Timmy;" "Did he hold the door for you?" "Well, he did and he didn't"). By learning to recognize verbal inconsistencies children can be encouraged to perceive inconsistencies involving actions for what they are.

Of course, not all inconsistencies are troublesome or unsettling. The clown who puts one foot up on a stool only to reach down and tie his other shoe and the comedian who swears that his next story is true are experts at presenting joyful inconsistencies. And soberminded philosophers have puzzled over special kinds of inconsistencies called paradoxes ever since the beginning of philosophy. Learning to recognize inconsistencies requires a growing awareness that a demand for consistency is not *always* appropriate; this involves recognition of when being inconsistent is confusing, misleading, and even deceptive, and when it is playful or profound.

d. *Discovering the feasibility of giving reasons for beliefs*

Let's say you've been having trouble getting to school on time. Your alarm clock's been broken and your car's battery has been run down. So now your principal asks you if you expect to be on time for the assembly program first thing tomorrow morning, and you reply, "I believe so."

The principal surprises you by asking you *why* you think you'll now be on time.

You answer, "Because my clock's been fixed, and I got a new battery for my car, and I can't think of any other reason why I'd be late."

You were challenged to give reasons for your belief, and you did.

Ordinarily, of course, no one challenges you to offer reasons for your beliefs.

But sometimes you can't help realizing that some belief of yours has just collapsed. Suppose that, tomorrow morning, fully believing that at last you're going to get to school on time, you're about to leave for work in your car, and discover you've got a flat tire. What happens to your belief that you're going to be on time? You can't continue to believe it, because there's no other means of transportation available. In other words, you've now got *no reason* to believe that you will be to work on time, so you can't continue to believe it. You may *hope,* of course, that just by chance someone will come along and give you a ride — but you have *no reason* to believe that anyone actually will.

Many of your actions and your thoughts are hinged upon your beliefs. You go to school each day in the belief that it's still there; you go home each day in the belief that *it's* still there. You wouldn't do many of the things you now do out of habit if you didn't believe things to be the way they are.

But this is all the more reason for your beliefs to be as sound as possible. And a good way to check up on their soundness is to be able to provide reasons or evidence for them. Your beliefs are the foundation of your whole outlook on life and of the way you live. Who would want the foundation of his beliefs to be shaky?

Think of it this way. If you were going to buy a house, you would certainly want to check around in the basement. It could be a very nice house, but it might rest on a very weak foundation, with water seeping everywhere and bricks crumbling away. Well, the same is true of your intellectual domicile: you want it to rest on solid foundations — and it can do so only if your belief-system is sound.

This is why it is helpful for children to challenge each other's ideas. Partly it's done out of playfulness; partly it's done out of competitiveness or contentiousness. (As with any game, there's always the possibility that it might get too rough for the individuals involved.) But it's a kind of dialogue that can be extremely beneficial, not just to the person asking the questions, but to the one thinking up the answers (that is, the person who is being challenged to provide reasons for believing as he does.) And it is helpful to the others who listen in and take note of what is going on: it will cause them to think a little more about why *they* believe as they do.

Always remember that, while the children who do most of the talking are invoking *their* right to express themselves, the children who sit by listening intently are thereby expressing *their* right to *hear* what is going on. And if you violate the right of the speaker by silencing him or her, you equally violate the rights of the listeners to hear what the speaker had to say. But, of course, you alone, as the teacher, are the judge of what is *relevant* to the class discussion and what is not. You should not hesitate to terminate a speaker who insists upon talking about irrelevant topics. To conclude:

1. It is a good thing to know your beliefs are sound and reliable, because you've got to act on them every day. If something goes wrong, you'd better check out your beliefs.
2. In a discussion, your beliefs may be challenged. You'll be asked to provide reasons for them. Thanks to previous discussions, you may be prepared to meet such requests.
3. You may have some good reasons for a particular belief, but they still may not be sufficient to justify your believing in that particular way. It's difficult to say just when reasons become numerous enough to be sufficient, but obviously, the more you can find, the better.

e. *Discovering comprehensiveness*

It's not enough for a person to have sound ideas on this subject and on that subject, a belief about this and a conviction about that, because all these little bits and pieces may not *add up* to anything. People generally *want* an organized set of beliefs and ideas for themselves, a body of thoughts and values that somehow are related and can be counted on in their future actions.

So young people have to be encouraged not merely to love and respect ideas, and not merely to want their ideas to be sound and reasonable. They have to be encouraged to see the connections *among* ideas as well — to see how ideas relate to one another, and converge upon one another and support one another. It's only in that way that a person can begin to build a network of thoughts that he will find permanently serviceable and useful.

As a teacher, you can be particularly helpful here. You have the experience of the world which children generally lack; you know a good deal about how things that go on in the world are related to one another. So you can guide children in this fashion by asking them if they can see the *connection* between certain ideas (where you believe you see a connection and they do not), and by helping them relate their ideas to things that happen in their lives and to the world in which they live. You can help them, when they seem to be groping, by suggesting connections and possible implications or consequences of their ideas. You can attempt to put their thoughts into some kind of context which will make their thoughts more meaningful to them, for the more comprehensive the setting of an idea is, the richer will that idea be in meaning.

Thus, you will notice that children are intensely conscious of each episode in the philosophical novels as they occur, but the very intensity of that awareness may block out their recollections of earlier incidents in the book. As a teacher, you can, through questioning, encourage them to see the *connections* between what went before and what came after. There is perhaps no better training that a child can have for the development of an adequate conception of self than to relate the present and the past and the future so as to see them as one continuous life.

As adults, we should try to be aware of how differently adults and children experience the world. A child usually feels the impact of a situation in its entirety, experiencing it as joyous, or miserable, as friendly or hostile, as threatening, or as inviting. But generally, the child does not analyze such a situation very much. Adults, on the other hand, having already learned relationships and connections that exist among things, perceive separate features of situations in isolation from one another.

The adult thus tends to think that the child should perceive the way the adult does by focusing on separate details until, part by part, he has put the situation together. What the child needs to be able to do, rather, is to explore it, discover what parts it contains, disentangle them from one another and understand their *connections* to one another. An adult who stresses beginning with the parts and ultimately arriving at the whole therefore runs directly contrary to the child's inclination to begin with the whole and subsequently discern its component parts.

In other words, children have a natural inclination to be speculative and comprehensive rather than analytic and sensitive to differences.

You as teacher cannot do better than to build upon this natural sense of wholeness which children demand, while at the same time helping them discover how it is put together.

f. *Discovering situations*

Much is heard these days about teaching children to make decisions, for it is assumed, at least in some quarters, that children ought to be decisive, the way police captains and quarterbacks and business executives are decisive. Now, there is no doubt that in a situation which calls for a choice to be made, the child should be able to make that choice as intelligently as possible. Surely if the child has the chance to choose — among different ypes of play, or different books to read, or different things to explore — and doesn't do so, then the child is not taking full advantage of the opportunities that are present.

On the other hand, if pressed to be decisive in situations where it would be better to wait and see how things develop, or until more facts are at hand, then the child can very well end up doing more harm than good by premature decisiveness. Very often, the child is presented with illustrative situations that are so skeletal or schematic, so lacking in specifics, that it would be very difficult for anyone to make a reasonable decision on the basis of the few facts promised. Yet, it is alleged that children are given practice in decision-making by being pressed to make up their minds as to what they would do in such artificial situations. But to exaggerate the importance of a decision is to exaggerate the product while neglecting the process. Children must be helped to grasp a situation in which the decision is required, and to read the character of that situation correctly. If the children have done so, the choice they have to make may be easier and will certainly be better due to their understanding of the situation's structure and requirements.

This program in philosophical thinking at times presents children with examples of moral situations. For instance, Dale has a problem as to whether or not to salute the flag, Ann treats her friend Suki as if she were an interesting object to bring home to her parents, Bill Beck throws a stone at Harry, Lisa accuses Mickey of stealing a briefcase. But it is not demanded of the children who read these problem situations that they say what they would do if they were the characters in the book. Rather, they are free to discuss, analyze, interpret and explore the complexities of these moral dilemmas. In this fashion, the children in the classroom can become more sensitive to the subtleties and nuances of the situations which they encounter in the book. And in the process, they may become more acutely aware of the moral character of situations which they encounter in their daily lives.

Philosophy is not a self-help course in decision-making. In fact, it might even make a decision harder to make by *widening* the range of alternatives from which to choose, rather than letting it stand as a decision between two courses of action.

Unless proper and adequate means for decision-making have already been developed in children, forcing a decision upon them, even an artificial or idealized one, is bound to be experienced as frustrating and perhaps even humiliating. We do not increase children's self-esteem when we force them into situations they are not prepared for; we lower it immeasurably.

What then are the *means* for the making of ethical judgments which must be developed in children? They are such things as respect for one another's point of view, the ability to identify sympathetically with other persons, the capacity to reason consistently, the capacity to imagine alternative possibilities, sensitivity to the variety of tiny but important factors which go to make up an interpersonal situation, and a feeling for the uniqueness of that particular situation and what would be right for *it*, even though roughly similar situations might have been treated differently in the past. Unless the children's development in these areas is carefully fostered and encouraged, they will find moral situations threatening and traumatic, and might well tend to avoid them.

Some devices that might prove very helpful would be to let the children act out (perhaps in pantomime, so as to give it the zany quality of a silent film), situations such as these: a woman with a lot of wild children getting on a crowded bus with an irritable bus driver; or an overworked pair of counter attendants at MacDonald's trying to handle a hungry bunch of vacationing school children; or a crowd's reaction to a tight-rope walker with an itch; or the family life of a teacher trying to grade papers at home while the teacher's own children tear up the house, watch television, grumble about doing the dishes, etc. There are countless such situations that can be improvised; what is important is for the children to identify with them and even to act them out without stressing the imperative that they make decisions: *Let the decision arrive, if it must, by flowing naturally and without fuss or self-consciousness out of the situation.* In short, it would be well to avoid making a big thing about decisions, and concentrate instead on preparing children for life situations by encouraging them to participate in imaginary ones where the emphasis is on getting them to perceive nuances of the situations, rather than on the choices that may *or may not* have to be made within each situation.

Children who have developed the capacity for sizing up situations, having an insight into their character, having imagination as to what can possibly be done to improve their unsatisfactory aspects, and having the courage to act on alternatives that seem to them most reasonable and plausible do not need a course in value-clarification or in decision-making, for they are already morally responsible individuals.

g. *Discovering part-whole relationships*

Try to imagine yourself in the school child's situation. There are many aspects of a school day which children find intensely meaningful. Perhaps foremost among these episodes of intense significance are those in which what one does is experienced as part of a larger picture.

For example, you are acting in a play. You have only a few lines to read. But what makes your part so important to you is that you see it as a part of the play as a whole. The meaning of the lines you are to read depend completely on what is said by the other actors in the play. You realize this so intensely that you may even learn all the parts, because to do so enables you to appreciate more fully the meaning of the whole and the meaning of your part in the whole.

Say you are part of the school baseball team. You may live for the moment you come to bat. But everyone knows the difference between being out on the field all by yourself with a bat and ball — a rather empty experience — and coming up to bat during a game that is full of excitement. Every player watches what every other player does and so each player empathizes with all the other players on both teams. In coming up to bat you sense how the outfielders are "playing you" and you sense the strategy the pitcher and the catcher have devised to pitch to you. At the same time, the other players on your team are living your experience at bat as if they were in your shoes. You have learned to sense everyone else's expectations of you. You grasp your role as a batter, in terms of the meaning to everyone involved in the game, and in terms of the relationship of your role to the game itself.

Or perhaps you are a member of the school orchestra. Your part in the school performance may be ever so slight, but it is indispensable. You may have but a single note to play on your instrument, but the entire piece of music would be seriously lacking if you failed to perform. So once again, each performance is appreciated by the player, the other members of the orchestra and by the audience as a totality in which each part is meaningful in terms of the ensemble in which it participates, and each work as an entirety derives its meaningfulness from the individual performances of which it is the composite.

Thus, there are many instances in the school day in which you learn part-whole relationships. Unfortunately, there are many other times during the ordinary school day in which what you are doing seems cut off from a larger picture, if there is one, and you don't seem to be able to understand what you are doing, or why you are doing it. In a well-integrated school day, there would be few such experiences. You would understand the relevance of each subject you take to your entire education, and you would understand each stage in the learning of each subject as necessary to the overall learning of that subject. You would appreciate the rationale behind alternating between intellectual and physical activity, between disciplined and innovative activity, between working with others and working by yourself, and between periods of actions and periods of reflection.

How does the understanding of part-whole relationships contribute to the attainment of the four objectives listed at the beginning of this chapter: a. improvement of reasoning ability; b. development of creativity; c. personal and interpersonal growth and d. development of ethical understanding?

a. If reasoning were taught simply as the principles and rules of logical inference, it would be an arid subject which would repel many students. If, on the other hand, the discovery of reasoning is presented in the setting of a children's novel, and if the reasoning then learned is shown to be valuable in the larger context of a person's life, the acquisition of the principles of reasoning can be much more attractive. This is not to say that learning and applying rules in a subject, simply as a kind of game which you can master, cannot be enjoyable in and of itself. But for many children it is hard to see principles of logic as a game, and as a result such children would find the study of logic quite joyless. Moreover, when children discover that reasoning learned in one class carries over to reasoning in other classes, that it is not confined to one subject area and is as useful in the playground and after school as it is in school, then the full impact of what they are doing in studying reasoning becomes very exciting.

b. The very definition of an aesthetic relationship is that of a relationship of parts to wholes (or of parts to other parts). To be engaged in art — to the fabricator of a work of art — is to be engaged in the organizing of parts into wholes. It is obvious that without sensitivity to this essential character of works of art, the children's development and their creative powers can be seriously hampered. It should be emphasized that younger children, between ages 2-7, display an easy proficiency in handling part-whole relationships, a proficiency which unfortunately tends to disintegrate as they move into pre-adolescence. At that later point, fussiness about details leads to lack of over-all organization, and a sense of proportion is often missing. One correlates this lack with the confusion in the child's mind at this time due to the loss of childhood patterns on the one hand, and the problematic patterns of adolescence confronting that child on the other hand. If the child's school day were replete with meaningful part-whole relationships, and if teachers in their teaching would pay particular attention to the relationship of fragments of knowledge to the larger context of the child's experience, then it is possible that the understanding of part-whole relationships would be cumulative rather than diminishing.

c. The confusion that a child feels about personal identity, life career, future life-style as an adult, family expectations, peer relationships, ambivalence toward education, and so on, can be dispelled only if the child is encouraged to reflect upon and analyze the basic direction of that child's own life. But how is this to be done? If philosophy for children were just a program in logic or critical thinking, then obviously it could not help the child dispel this confusion. But it is much more than that. It involves dialogue concerning issues and concepts of which children are struggling to make sense, coupled with an exposure to alternative views that have been created by philosophers in the past. Children are told to be natural, but what is it to be natural? They are told to be themselves, but who are they? They are encouraged to learn and respect the customs of society, but what are customs?

Children experience a need to reflect upon the key aspects of that period of life experience through which they are passing at the moment. We err in thinking that we can sweep away the child's problems simply by giving the child little recipes for expeditious social or personal behavior, when the child cannot understand the terms in the recipe. Adults offer explanations or issue injunctions to children while taking for granted that the children understand the terms and concepts involved in those explanations and injunctions. But this cannot be taken for granted. The child senses that the language and concepts adults employ in presenting a view of the world or in presenting a directive for how the child should act in that world — that such language and concepts form an intimate part of the adult world view. The philosophy of life which an older generation would like a younger generation to accept becomes suspect to that younger generation by virtue of the terms in which the philosophy of life is couched. This is why children constantly want to know what we mean when we use this term or that term: they are concerned not with just the words themselves, but with the beliefs in which those terms are embedded, and which they are not prepared to adopt without further explanation. Philosophy for children is serious about encouraging children to think for themselves, and it will help them discover the rudiments of their own philosophy of life. In so doing it helps children develop a more secure sense of their own identities.

d. At the beginning of this section we offered illustrations of part-whole relationships involving a play, a baseball game and a musical performance. In each of these instances there is an explicit or implicit understanding of what it means for behavior to be *right* in such contexts. The drama director will object to an actor's reading of a certain line by saying, "No, that won't do, that's not right at all!" The batting coach will explain to a rookie player the difference between the wrong and the right way to use one's body in swinging a bat. The orchestral conductor will criticize the way a group of instrumentalists have played a certain section of a piece over and over again, but then the conductor will say of a performance: "That's it, that's *right*, now you've got it." It is very instructive that everyone concerned can understand and appreciate the appropriateness of the use of the word *right* in this fashion. It is in each instance understood that what is right is not right in itself, but is right in terms of the relationship between an act and the entire context of which it is a part.

In encouraging children to develop an ethical understanding, we must help them see the relationship between what they propose to do and the situation in which they propose to do it. They should be encouraged to see that relationship as they would look at any part whose appropriateness to an entire context must be judged. Thus, children must be sensitized to the ethical aspects of situations in such a way that they begin to sense that what they are doing is appropriate or inappropriate as they prepare to act on them. Such appropriateness, as in the illustrations of the play, the baseball game and the musical performance, can be judged "right," at least for the moment. Further consideration of consequences of a particular act (to others, to oneself, to institutions of one's society) may lead one to modify one's initial judgment. But a keen awareness of the general outlines of a moral situation, and a feeling for how a proposed action would fit into that configuration (as "rightly" or "wrongly") is the kind of awareness that must be one of the major objectives of an ethical education.

In so far as the philosophy for children program stresses the cultivation of part-whole understanding, it contributes effectively to the development of the child as an ethical individual.

Chapter Five

TEACHING

METHODOLOGY

1. GETTING CHILDREN TO THINK FOR THEMSELVES

Encouraging children to think philosophically is not an easy task for teachers to master. In many ways, it is more of an art than a technique—an art comparable to leading an orchestra or directing a play. And since, like any art, it takes practice, you should not allow yourself to be discouraged the first or second time you use the philosophy for children curriculum.

As you go through the course with your students, you will learn how important to its success is proper timing in the introduction and sequential presentation of materials. Teaching philosophy involves eliciting themes from students and then repeatedly returning to them, weaving them into the fabric of the students' discussions as the classes proceed. If one looks at the curriculum for grades 5-8, one will notice that the themes in *Harry Stottlemeier's Discovery* and *Lisa* are introduced and then occur again and again, each time in a little more depth, breadth and sophistication. Unlike 'atomistic' teaching, which introduces a segment of knowledge, drills for it until it is mastered by the students, and then moves on to something new, this 'organic' approach to teaching touches lightly on philosophical concepts in the beginning and then slowly builds a deeper understanding of the same concepts as they relate to recurrent motifs.

As you review *Harry Stottlemeier's Discovery* and *Lisa,* you will see that this approach to teaching is embedded in the novels themselves. The two books are works of fiction in which the characters eke out for themselves the laws of reasoning and the discovery of alternative philosophical views that have been presented through the centuries. The method of discovery for each of the children in the novels is dialogue coupled with reflection. This dialogue with peers, with teachers, with parents, grandparents and relatives, alternating with reflections upon what has been said, is the basic vehicle by which the characters in the stories come to learn. And it is how your students will likewise come to learn—by talking and thinking things out.

This is not to imply that the role of the teacher is non-existent or minimal—that the learning occurs just by letting the children discuss the novel day after day. Nor does it imply that somehow the knowledge is already there, "in the children," as it were, so that all one need do is put pupils together in a room and it will all come out. On the contrary, it is assumed that philosophical learning occurs primarily through interaction between the children and their environment — and that environment consists primarily of the physical classroom, other children, parents, relatives, friends, people in the community, the media and the teacher.

However, it is the teacher who, at least in the classroom, can manipulate the environment in such a way as to enhance the possibility that the children will continually grow in philosophical awareness. It is the teacher who can elicit the themes in each of the chapters in the philosophical novels, who can point out themes the students in the classroom fail to identify, who can relate the themes to the children's experience when they seem to be having trouble doing so on their own, who can manifest by everyday behavior how philosophy can make a difference in one's immediate life—how it can open up horizons that make each day more meaningful. Further, it is the teacher who, through questioning, can introduce alternative views with the aim of always enlarging the students' horizons, never letting complacency or self-righteousness take precedence. In this sense, the teacher is a gadfly, encouraging the students take the initiative, building on what they manage to formulate, helping them question underlying assumptions of what they arrive at, and suggesting ways of arriving at more comprehensive answers. In order to be successful, the teacher must not only know philosophy, but know how to introduce this knowledge at the right times in a questioning, wondering way that supports the children in their own struggle for understanding.

Naturally, there are certain underlying assumptions about the nature of the mind and how a child learns embedded in the philosophy for children program. Rather than envisaging the mind as an empty passive vessel which must be stuffed with information or content in order to be 'educated,' it is assumed that children learn by being actively involved in exploration. Further, it is presumed that knowledge is not simply learned by rote but is something mastered by interacting with the environment, and by solving problems important to children. The knowledge is theirs when they can show, through their discussions and through their actions, that they can apply it to what they are doing, whether it is figuring out a syllogism or dealing with an interpersonal conflict on the playground. It is not theirs if they can say the words but are unable to use the knowledge the words express. Philosophy is empty if reduced to a memorization of "who said what, and when" or "how one philosophical view compares with another" as ends in themselves. It takes on significance only when children begin to manifest the capacity to think for themselves and to figure out their own answers about life's important issues. As philosophy opens up alternative possibilities for individuals' leading qualitatively better lives—richer and more meaningful lives—it gains a growing place in the school curriculum.

So that children can come to grips with ideas and not merely with labels, no mention is made of philosophers' names in the philosophy for children program (although their ideas are certainly introduced), and you as a teacher would be better off not using these names in class. In due time, the children will discover whose ideas they originally were, but this should happen only after authentically grappling with the ideas in trying to make sense of their experience, in trying to enlarge their own horizons, and thus in coming to understand themselves and others in a more comprehensive way.

2. CONDITIONS FOR TEACHING PHILOSOPHICAL THINKING

Children cannot be expected to engage productively in philosophical discussion unless these important conditions obtain in your classroom:

   Commitment to philosophical inquiry

   Avoidance of indoctrination

   Respect for children's opinions

   Evocation of children's trust

a. *Commitment to philosophical inquiry*
The philosophy for children curriculum is in no way designed to be

61

teacher-proof. More than anything, philosophical inquiry among children is dependent on a teacher who understands children, is sensitive to philosophical issues, and is capable of manifesting in everyday behavior a deep commitment to philosophical inquiry—not as an end in itself but as a means for leading a qualitatively better life. Teachers who can model an endless quest for meaning—for more comprehensive answers to life's important issues—are the most important ingredient in the philosophy for children program. This commitment is evidenced in their integrity, their having and acting on principles, and their manifesting a consistency between what they say and what they do.

The teaching of philosophy consists in recognizing and following very closely what children are thinking, helping them to verbalize and objectify these thoughts and then aiding the development of the tools they need to reflect upon these thoughts. But this role is impossible unless the teachers themselves are models of persons who believe that, in the end, *it makes a difference to do this.* The effective teacher of philosophy ultimately must communicate a passion for excellence in thinking, excellence in creating, excellence in conduct—values that students may glimpse in the process of philosophical dialogue.

Remember, the commitment you are encouraging on the child's part is commitment to *the process of inquiry itself,* whether this be logical, aesthetic, scientific or moral inquiry. The child should eventually be able to distinguish between your idiosyncratic values and the process that you try to embody. While there will be times when you will stray, it is that process to which you will most repeatedly return.

b. Avoidance of Indoctrination

One goal of education is the liberation of students from unquestioning, uncritical mental habits, in order that they may better develop the ability to think for themselves, to discover their own orientation to the world and, when ready to do so, to devise their own set of beliefs about it. We cannot expect children to respect themselves as persons unless they have learned to utilize fully the intellectual and creative powers with which they are equipped. Every child should be encouraged to develop and articulate his or her own way of looking at things. Different children have different values. But if they hold these values thoughtfully, if they have given consideration to why they feel and think the way they do, if they have given some reflection to their needs and interests and activities, this will be an indication that their philosophical discussions have been helpful for them. It doesn't particularly matter whether they turn out to have different ways of looking at things. It doesn't particularly matter that they disagree with one another or with the teacher on philosophical issues. What matters most is that they get a better understanding of what they think and why they think and feel and act the way they do, and of how it might be to reason effectively.

There is no study which can more effectively prepare the child to combat indoctrination than philosophy. No discipline offers children the range of alternatives to questions of utmost importance to them, nor does any other discipline take more seriously the development of their capacity to judge for themselves. But the power and authority of philosophy carries with it great responsibility.

No course in philosophical thinking, whether for children or adults, can succeed if used as a means for implanting the teacher's values in the vulnerable minds of the children in the classroom. No matter that the teacher is confident his values are the "correct" ones; if this is what he is doing, it is the destruction of philosophy.

On the other hand, there are teachers who feel they must be very careful not to reveal any values of their own in their teaching. They believe that their method of teaching is and must remain "value free." But such teachers may be deceiving themselves as well as their students. For no educational process is completely value free. All teachers reveal their values in what they say and do, if only through inflections of voice, gestures or facial expressions, the way they conduct a class or give a test. Teachers of philosophical thinking must therefore beware at all times of wittingly or unwittingly encouraging children to adopt their own personal set of values in an uncritical fashion. Nor can they escape the fact that children not unreasonably look up to those whose experience of the world is broader or deeper than their own. The teacher's attitudes, whatever they be, are bound to carry considerable weight with youngsters who are unsure of the significance of their own experience.

Students engaged in philosophical discussion should feel free to advocate any value position they choose, without the teacher's having to agree or disagree with each and every point. Teachers who persistently interpose their own views run the risk, if not of indoctrination, at least of creating inhibitions which will sooner or later close off discussion itself. Only when students have developed to the point where they are able to deal objectively with the teacher's opinions and not be coerced by them, can the teacher contribute his own opinions to the discussion—provided the students want to know what they are.

A question naturally arises at this point concerning the teacher's insistence that participants in philosophical discussions try to be coherent, consistent and comprehensive in their thinking: "Aren't coherence, consistency and comprehensiveness simply replacements for the personal values which the teacher is being asked not to force upon his students?" There are two answers to this question.

a. Coherence, consistency and comprehensiveness are values only in the sense that they are standards for effective communication, and criteria for effective inquiry. They are appropriate to *the way* a person should think, not to *what* he should think. Therefore, they are *procedural* considerations, not *substantive ones.*

b. There are other forms of activity in which these rules are hindrances rather than aids. For example, the children may find that their play need not be consistent, that the chores they do at home need not be comprehensive, and that their poetic impulses are stifled if it is demanded that they be more coherent. In other words, coherence, comprehensiveness and consistency are appropriate values for philosophical discussion and inquiry but not for other aspects of a person's life which include characteristics of spontaneity, randomness, or routine to which the aforementioned values are irrelevant.

However, this still does not fully answer the question of indoctrination and philosophy. A further question may be raised: "Is it not indoctrination to teach children logic?" Our answer must be that such instruction does involve a degree of risk. Certainly there are kinds of formal logic other than the Aristotelian logic which one finds in *Harry Stottlemeier's Discovery* and *Lisa,* and there are various other approaches to non-formal logic as well. It cannot even be said that the child who learns logic will necessarily draw correct inferences, since logic apparently helps us very little to improve our psychological processes. Rather, by providing us with criteria by which to evaluate the inferences that we do make, logic helps us distinguish better from worse ways of reasoning. It may not eliminate our mistakes, but at least it helps us recognize them.

There is nothing final about logical criteria. They are like parliamentary rules of discussion which are agreed to in carrying on a debate. As you know, even a classroom discussion cannot proceed unless there are some implicit or explicit agreements as to ground rules such as "no irrelevant talk will be permitted," "no filibustering," "no use of force," etc. Similarly, logic sets ground rules for rational dialogue.

Teaching logic is not a form of indoctrination, inasmuch as logic is employed as an instrument for appraising the inferences we draw. We recognize that the grammar of a particular language is a device by means of which it is possible to distinguish speaking well from speaking badly. It is no more indoctrination to insist that children be logical in their thinking than to insist that they be grammatical in their speech. Moreover, as we have already pointed out, there will be, on occasion, considerable value in forms of reasoning generally thought of as invalid. Just as a novelist may have excellent reasons for

64

choosing to be ungrammatical, a poet may have excellent reasons for choosing to be illogical. What the teacher must seek to convey is that *in certain contexts* and *for certain purposes,* it is beneficial to be able to speak grammatically and think logically.

The question may nevertheless be asked whether the philosophy for children program might be indoctrinational with respect to areas of philosophy other than logic. In other words, does the program contain a "hidden agenda?" Is there some underlying set of values upon which the whole program is predicated?

To respond to these questions, we must recognize that any educational program is necessarily founded upon certain explicit or implicit assumptions. We assume, for example, that the process of education has much in common with the process of inquiry. We believe that at every stage of a child's development free inquiry can be fostered in ways that will be wholesome and constructive both for the child and for society. Just how far inquiry is to be promoted for a given child at a given age is not altogether clear and to a great extent will depend upon the tact and sensitivity of the teacher. But the objective of our program for children of all ages is the liberation of those of their powers which are destructive of neither the children themselves nor of other people. Free inquiry provides an incomparable framework for such development.

c. *Respect for children's opinions*

Respect for children's opinions assumes that the teacher in many ways has a philosophical view of knowledge itself. If you think you already know all the answers, if you think you have a direct line to the truth, then it will be rather hard for you to respect childrens' opinions (or adult opinions for that matter) should they differ from your own. However, if you realize that you are still searching for more comprehensive answers in all of the educational disciplines as well as in your own personal life, and further, if you realize that knowledge itself is endlessly being created by human beings to explain the world they live in, then you will be more apt to listen to all people, including children, for ideas that might lead to more comprehensive and meaningful explanations than you now possess.

If you have been teaching for a while, you may have experienced the remarkable capacity for insight that children often manifest. Whether it is their lack of socialization, with all of its categorization and set ways of looking at the world, or their lack of inhibition, children often display a remarkable ability to approach problems in a fresh way. And often this insight on their part is a clue to a sounder formulation of the issue.

In addition, even if a child expresses an opinion that you are sure is not based on factual knowledge, your commitment to that child's growth should be your guide to action. Rather than "putting children down," it would be more productive to try to establish a mutual relationship of trust and empathy which might get them to admit that they do not know all the answers and that, like you, they experience the world as confusing and frustrating at times. Once this happens, one can begin the slow process of helping them to clarify their own views, getting them to see what such views imply in terms of assumptions and consequences, exposing them to alternatives, and giving them the tools they need to think for themselves about matters that concern them.

d. *Evocation of children's trust.*

As for the matter of trust, it not only is indispensable to encouraging children to think philosophically, but is the foundation of sound teacher-student relationships. Most children are extremely sensitive to the whole spectrum of techniques which enable an adult to condescend to children and humiliate them. A slight or a "put down" will have only a momentary shock, but it leaves a scar, and that scar means that the trust essential to the learning process has been lost. Some people evoke immediate trust from others. But most of us have to work at it patiently. And there is no infallible recipe as to how one does it.

We should distinguish three kinds of classroom situations. Most undesirable, of course, is the classroom in which the students are afraid to "open up" before the teacher because they fear the loss of affection or respect. Somehow the teacher has not communicated that he respects them for what they are, whether they agree or disagree with him.

A better situation is one in which the students feel free to discuss abstract matters, but are very careful not to say or imply anything that would challenge the values they believe the teacher to hold. Again, somehow, the teacher has communicated that his view are not to be challenged if one is to "stay within his good graces." This communication (typically non-verbal) can constitute a serious impediment to the student's philosophical growth.

The optimum situation obviously is one in which the students trust the teacher sufficiently to risk criticism of the teacher's methods or values, because they know the teacher will consider such criticisms from them fairly. A teacher who respects his students is ready always to learn from them, and somehow in his behavior makes this known to them. He will be able to recognize that their sometimes critical or mischievous comments are their ways of testing him for his reactions. The teacher who is himself insecure or defensive and who finds criticism from children intolerable will quickly be spotted by the children as someone whom they are not prepared to trust. Thus it follows that a teacher who is insecure or defensive about his own opinions, who, for one reason or another either holds his views rigidly or dogmatically, or is defensive about his way of arriving at them, is not likely to be able to encourage children to think philosophically.

This in no way condones student disrespect. However, respect is a two-way street, and teachers who do not respect their students, their opinions, their needs and their interests, and who do not manifest this respect in their behavior every day in the classroom, are unrealistic if they think their students are going to respect them just because they are teachers.

3. HOW IS THE METHODOLOGY OF PHILOSOPHY FOR CHILDREN RELATED TO THE TRAINING OF TEACHERS THEMSELVES?

In the time since you began teaching, it is likely that you have more than once reflected upon the sharp differences between the way you were taught a subject when you were in college and the way in which you have to present it to your pupils in order that they find it comprehensable. Your professors in college probably organized the material of the discipline in a carefully structured way that one would use for writing a course outline — with headings, sub-headings and further sub-headings. But you soon discovered that such an organization of materials was likely to impress your own pupils as arid, stilted and baffling.

If you tried different ways of presenting such materials to children, you may have found that one of the most successful was to begin with that portion of the material which seemed most naturally suited to their interests. But what next? Your next step would be to find another portion of the subject that would meet two conditions: it should follow logically from the first bit of information, but at the same time it should once again be of interest to your students. The third area to be introduced would likewise meet these two requirements, and so on until you had systematically covered the syllabus you had set for yourself, yet each presentation would have been attuned to the *developing* interest and reflective curiosity of the child. This reorganization of the academically organized material as taught in college into an arrangement so sequenced as constantly to satisfy, challenge, delight or stimulate the child is essential to the presentation of material in the classroom.

There is no doubt that if you carry over into your classroom the methodology to which you probably were exposed in college (which presented the material to you in accordance with its *logical* structure), your success in philosophy for children will be seriously jeopardized. We have made an attempt to take much of the burden from you by reconstructing the philosophical material in such a way that it should appeal to the students in your class in a sequential and cumulatively enlarging fashion. But this is not to say that there will be no need for you to rework and reorganize the approach of handling each of the chapters in a way that fits in with the interests and the abilities of the students in your class. The course material is designed to allow you as a teacher the maximum flexibility in adapting the material to your students' needs.

You will notice in the Instructional Manual accompanying each of the philosophical novels that each chapter contains a list of some of the noteworthy ideas in that chapter, a commentary on these ideas, and exercises and activities designed both to reinforce these leading motifs and show their relation to the other disciplines that the child studies during the day.

You might begin a particular lesson by asking your students what they thought were the most important ideas and events in the chapter, and move on from there to unpacking the chapter with your students' help. This analysis is really an in-depth explanation of the text, of which the leading ideas are merely a skeletal framework. It is when the concepts are analyzed and related to the students' own lives that they begin to take on more and more meaning. As the course proceeds, you will probably find that the children will be able to spend a longer and longer period of time on each of the chapters, extracting more and more personal and interpersonal meaning from them. And the instructional manual should aid you to guide your pupils in that direction. But only you will know how much and when, and that sense of timing will grow as you get to know your material and your students more fully.

Other days you might want to begin with one of the activities that aims at clarifying one of the central themes in the chapter, but at the same time relates that theme to the social studies or science or language arts the children have been studying that week. Giving each of the students an opportunity to engage in the activity either on an individual or group basis for a portion of the lesson might create a meaningful interpersonal experience that would throw light on the remainder of the chapter.

Other days you might begin by asking your pupils if they can figure out why a certain character (say, Millie) did what she did in that chapter. What do we know about this character from the previous chapters that would help to explain her behavior? Do you remember in Chapter Two that she seems to have shown the same pattern of behavior? Why does she conduct herself in this fashion with this particular friend? Has she always acted this way toward her friend? If not, what happened previously that might explain why she did what she did? What kind of a relationship do they seem to have? Is the relationship growing in understanding on both of their parts, or does the friend seem to understand her better than she understands her friend?

Questions such as these can trigger an analysis of the different characters in the novels that will aid the students not only to interpret the novel in a more comprehensive manner, but also to gain a deeper insight into people — why they do the things they do, and how others in their environment affect this behavior. As you relate and interrelate the actions in one chapter with the actions of the characters in the previous chapters, you not only aid the students to gain a more holistic view of the work itself, but a deeper understanding of how the characters in the novel slowly grow in philosophical awareness as they discover the nature of reasoning, and as they discover alternative views about issues that mean a great deal to them. You may find that some of the children in your class identify with a character in the novel and eventually will want to say why. You may find that some students seem to understand one of the characters much more than the others. Eventually this can lead to an analysis of the uniqueness of each of the characters in the story, their different styles of thinking, playing, and acting. As the class proceeds, and you get to know each other better, you may find that your students are slowly becoming more and more sensitive to the subtleties of each character's behavior in each of the chapters, and will want to discuss these nuances in class.

4. TEACHING BEHAVIOR CONDUCIVE TO HELPING CHILDREN ENGAGE IN PHILOSOPHICAL THINKING

Everyone is familiar with the sign THINK, and just about everyone realizes that the sign doesn't encourage thinking at all; if anything, it inhibits it. Ideas cannot be produced on command. What *can* be done is to create an atmosphere hospitable to good thinking, and to recognize that children have very diverse styles of mental behavior, each one of which needs nurturing in a somewhat different fashion.

In this sense, thinking is an art, and every artist proceeds somewhat differently. The teacher of any art must be able to discern the creative dispositions of the child and encourage their fulfillment. Likewise with teaching philosophy, the teacher must be prepared to nurture and cultivate a rich profusion of thinking styles, yet all the while insisting upon each child's thought being as clear, consistent and comprehensive as possible so long as the *content* of the child's thought is not compromised. If teachers of philosophy would keep in mind this similarity of philosophy to the arts, and keep in mind that the proper role of the teacher is to encourage intellectual creativity as well as intellectual rigor, they will be safeguarded from concluding that all

69

children are going to approach *Harry Stottlemeier's Discovery* and *Lisa* in the same way.

Surely, if you visited an art class and found all the students painting alike, you would suspect that the teacher had misunderstood the nature of art education, and instead of encouraging creativity was seeking to produce uniform works of art as well as uniform children. So it is with the teaching of philosophy. To visit a philosophy class and discover that everyone in it had developed the same point of view would suggest that something is amiss somewhere. Different people have different styles of thought; they have different life experiences, different goals and objectives, and it is plausible to expect from them a rich variety of philosophical perspectives.

It is up to the teacher to encourage just this variety of philosophical insights and approaches. What is held in common in philosophy are means — rather than ends. That is, philosophy insists upon reasonable dialogue, but only as a means by which students can arrive at their own points of view and their own conclusions. Philosophy insists upon logical rigor, but only as a means of making thinking more efficient, which is quite different from having everyone's ideas conform to everyone else's.

Thus, your role is to help children master such means as the rules of logical inference and the etiquette of classroom discussion. It is not your role to dictate to children what their philosophies of life should be. In this sense, take your cue from *Harry Stottlemeier* and *Lisa*. The children in those books struggle to understand, hold their views fairly tentatively, are open to new suggestions, and are committed to the kind of communal inquiry in which individuals learn from one another as well as from their own experience. To the extent to which you can encourage your students to identify with these procedures, you will not have to worry about getting the children to think, because they will embark upon the process wholeheartedly and of their own volition.

a. *Maintaining relevance*

Just as thinking is an art, so teaching is an art, and a considerable portion of the art of teaching relates to the teacher's awareness of what is and is not relevant to an ongoing philosophical discussion. Normally, it is not too difficult to distinguish between comments that relate to a discussion and comments that are irrelevant. But there is a grey area in between, in which a teacher must exercise a considerable amount of discretion. Children in the age bracket of 10-14 are often prone to introducing personal experiences into the discussion, some very psychological in nature. The teacher has an option here of allowing such remarks to focus the discussion on the child's personal difficulty, as over against allowing the comment to serve as an *illustration* of a broader treatment of the issue. In the first case, the danger is clear that the discussion may become not a matter of philosophy but a matter of psychological therapy. The classroom is not the place for such therapy and neither the teacher nor the child's peers are the individuals to conduct it.

On the other hand, there is nothing wrong with a child's sharing a concern or giving an autobiographical account of some experience, where the teacher recognizes that this can be deftly directed towards an objective and impartial understanding by everyone in the class of the philosophical issues involved on which the personal account just related is able to shed light. In this case, the personal account serves to illustrate a broad philosophical issue which all the children in the class can benefit from exploring, whereas in the case cited earlier, the attention of the children is merely directed to the personal account itself.

Suppose a boy mentions that he was teased by girls. Now this can be an opportunity for the teacher to try to deal with this one specific instance — and it may turn out to be another humiliating experience for the boy. One way that the discussion can go is an exploration of why the teasing occurred — whether he deserved it, whether he did anything to the girls yesterday, and so on. Another direction that the discussion can take, if the teacher guides it carefully, is into a discussion of teasing itself; what, if anything, it accomplishes, why people tease other people, and what teasing may be a symptom of. Ultimately, the discussion can open up the broad philosophical question of what fairness is. But this will not frequently happen unless the teacher plays a guiding role, gently moving the discussion away from the specific, and in the direction of the general.

Children at this age level may want to share views about sex, about what is right and wrong, about their relationships with their families, and other such matters. The important thing for the teacher to realize is that these topics may well be fertile ground for a philosophical discussion, but only if the movement of the discussion is away from the intensely private and personal aspects of the account, and towards the more inclusive, comprehensive and constructive aspects of the problem. A philosophical discussion is profitable if it moves from what is to what could be, or from the special case to a broader understanding. It is not a philosophical discussion if children merely get their personal problems off their chests, or express themselves emotionally, or use the hour as an opportunity to regale one another with litanies of alleged injustices, or seek attention by telling personal anecdotes. But these accounts can be starting points for a philosophical discussion in the hands of the able teacher. It is up to the teacher to determine whether the account has philosophical implications, what the implicit philosophical themes are, and to guide the children gradually into a discussion of these themes.

When a teacher hears one child say to another "you're retarded," (or "sick," or "unfair" or "gross") these are opportunities for seeking to discover the criteria by which we determine what is healthy, what is fair or what is beautiful. In other words, what the teacher is trying to achieve is to get the children to make explicit, when they use such terms as "sick," "unfair," "unjust," what *their criteria* are for making such statements — what standards they use for making such observations. As the discussion begins to revolve around such criteria and standards, you, the teacher, know that you are on solid ground.

Ultimately, the teacher is the one who has to make the judgment as to whether a particular personal account should be capitalized upon or squelched. On the one hand, a child's wish to contribute may be repetitive, redundant, superfluous, or symptomatic of a need to dominate the discussion in an unproductive way. On the other hand, it may be something which, although anecdotal, is very rich in the implications that it suggests for a broader insight into the problem at issue for all members of the class.

The children in the classroom are likely to be very attentive to the manner in which the teacher operates in this zone of discretion — between what is clearly relevant and what is clearly irrelevant. In a very short time they will be testing and challenging to see just how personal, how anecdotal, how subjective they can be without causing the teacher to respond negatively. If they have had experiences where the teacher has capitalized on their accounts and moved them into a philosophical discussion, they will probably want to have such experiences again. If, on the other hand, they find that the teacher will put up with aimless discussion, they'll continue to ramble on pointlessly until they get bored.

b. *Questioning*

Like many children, the students in your class are probably imaginative, curious and intellectually lively. The chances are that, like many children, they'll become increasingly less thoughtful and less reflective as they grow up. The change is gradual, day by day, that one hardly notices the loss. Slowly the brightness fades, and the potential dribbles away. Suddenly you may some day begin to see that they are becoming unimaginative, unquestioning, uncritical in their behavior.

No doubt you want your students to be able to think, and to think for themselves. You want them to be rational and responsible individuals. You hope they'll find their lives meaningful rather than empty. But when it comes to encouraging them to reason, when it comes to

72

encouraging them to look for meaning in what happens to them and in what they do, you may well feel very helpless.

Children need models with which to identify. They need models of leadership if they are to see themselves as future leaders. They need models of integrity if they are to realize what it means to be honest. And they need models of intelligent adult-child conversation if they are to believe in the possibility of dialogue.

To help children learn to think for themselves, to move in the direction of becoming independent, resourceful, self-sufficient individuals, ask yourself, "What good is served by my readily providing children with answers every time they ask questions?" "What good is accomplished by their memorizing information from textbooks without trying to understand the concepts involved or the underlying presuppositions?" "Do I myself serve children as a model of an individual who constantly questions, who seeks always for more sufficient answers, who is more interested in dialogue and discovery than memorization of facts?"

In *Lisa*, we encounter a model of an adult-child conversation which can be one of mutual discovery for both adult and child, while at the same time we gain some insight into the nature of questions.

> "Dad," said Harry.
> "Mmmm," said his father.
> "Dad," Harry repeated.
> "Hmmm?" his father answered.
> "Dad, what's a question?"
> "What you're asking me."
> "Yeah, I know I'm asking you a question, but that's not the question I'm asking you."
> "What's the question you're asking me? We seem to be going round and round, like Abbott and Costello. Who's on first?"
> "Dad!"
> "What?"
> "I'm serious. What's a question?"
> "Why do you want to know?"
> "Dad, that's beside the point. What difference does it make why I want to know? I just want to know."
> "You're always asking why. Why can't I ask why?"
> "Dad, all I asked you was a simple question and you go round and round. All I was trying to find out was, what happens when we ask a question?"

The conversation proceeds guardedly and somewhat painfully on both sides. But there is a sense of progress. Eventually Harry remarks that maybe a person who asks a question has a problem. Then, pondering his own remark for a moment, he asks, "Is that what you're telling me, that we ask questions because we've got problems?"

> "Do we have problems or do the problems have us?"
> "Oh, Dad, for gosh sake, will you be serious?"
> "I am serious."

73

"Well, what's the connection between a question and a problem?"

"What's the connection between an iceberg and the tip of the iceberg."

"The tip of the iceberg is all you can see; the rest of it is under water."

"So isn't it possible that your question is just the tip of the problem?"

"The question's mine, but the problem's not mine?"

"Could be."

"So whose is it?"

"It doesn't have to be anybody's. Look, if you were finished with school and you weren't sure what you were going to do next, you'd be puzzled, and you'd start asking questions. But if there weren't any jobs, then that's a problem, and it's not just *your* problem. That's why I said, you wouldn't have it, but it would have you."

"So the reason I ask questions is not so much to get answers, as to get to know what the problem is?"

"Mr. Stottlemeier touched Harry's head lightly with his hand.

"I couldn't have put it better myself," he said.

Now, not all children are as persistently inquisitive as is Harry Stottlemeier in this novel. But when teachers are skilled in cultivating their students' thinking through questioning themselves, the end result is children who can think for themselves about everything in their own experience. Children want to think about such things as who they are, why they are made to go to school, what their minds are, what death is, what things are right or wrong to do, etc. So why not begin there — with their problems?

The art of questioning is very complex. Naturally, there are some questions which deserve answers. If a child asks you where the library is, you may as well tell him. But quite different is a question asking you what the meaning of a word is, when you both know that there are several dictionaries in the room. Likewise, if a child asks you a philosophical question, such as "what is fair?" and you respond by telling him how you would define it, there is a danger that you are foreclosing the very kind of inquiry which his question is intended to open up — the kind of inquiry which is the very foundation of thinking for oneself.

For example, this conversation was overheard recently in a sixth grade class in philosophy:

Teacher:	"Why do you go to school?"
First Pupil:	"To get an education."
Teacher:	"What is an education?"
Second Pupil:	"Having all the answers."
Teacher:	"Do educated people have all the answers?"
Third Pupil:	"Sure, they do."
Teacher:	"Am I educated?"
First Pupil:	"Sure."
Teacher:	"Do I have all the answers?"

74

Third Pupil:	"I don't know. You're always asking us questions."
Teacher:	"So I'm grown up and educated but I ask questions. And you're kids and you give answers, right?"
Second Pupil:	"You mean, the more educated we become, the more we ask questions instead of give answers? Is that it?"
Teacher:	"What do you think?"

Teachers who pretend to be all-knowing do a double disservice to their students. First, by supplying them with answers that they should discover for themselves, such teachers fail to prepare their students for the day when adult support will not be present, and they will be left to their own undeveloped resources. Or, when the day comes that the model of omniscience collapses, when children find out that the teacher doesn't have all the answers, their security and trust may be shattered, and once again they are helpless because they have not been encouraged to develop the tools they need to find their own answers. Secondly, such teachers create in their pupils the model or ideal of the educated person as all-knowing, rather than as a person who is intellectually open, curious, self-critical and willing to admit ignorance or indecision.

Further, when the teacher pretends to be all-knowing, the child comes away with the view that knowledge is answers — something outside of oneself to be memorized — rather than something to be discovered and created. Instead of involving the child in the process of knowledge-acquiring, the teacher with all the answers (or the teacher who insists on children regurgitating answers) has deprived such children of the very joy that will stand them in good stead in later years — the satisfaction of finding answers for themselves. The connection between this satisfaction and being an imaginative, curious and intellectually lively person is very substantial.

Remember that children constantly use you as their model of sound intellectual bearing, and they identify with your behavior. If you want to strengthen their curiosity, display to them the image of a mature yet questioning adult. Such an image confirms children in their freedom to explore, to ask further questions, to investigate the various alternatives available, and finally to arrive at some tentative answers. The capacity to hold one's answers as tentative rather than as dogma is something children can learn readily from you. But, if you present the image of someone who has all the answers, with the implication that these answers are the 'right' answers, you present the image of someone who knows it all and thus you discourage children's exploring, questioning and searching for more comprehensive solutions.

When you ask children "Why?," you challenge them to dig deeper into their own assumptions, to make better use of their own intellectual resources, to come up with more imaginative and creative proposals than they would have if your stance towards them were that of a supplier of facts. Even if there are situations in which giving answers is appropriate, there are ways of doing so which open up the issue more and invite children's inquiry instead of closing it off.

This characteristic of questioning, which is essential to encouraging children to think philosophically, is manifested not only in how you answer children, but in the way you engage in teaching throughout the day. If you encourage children to accept answers, to be uncritical, to memorize facts that they don't understand, if you concentrate your energies on giving tests which do not draw upon their creativity or their active understanding, your students are likely to acquire the impression that they become more educated as they assimilate more facts. And this is hardly the best way to conceive of education.

Finally, you should not be afraid to challenge those assumptions which children make *even though you may happen to agree with them,* if the result promises to be a livelier attitude on the child's part towards the material. For example, you might have this kind of discussion:

Pupil: "When was George Washington born?"
Teacher: "Why don't you look it up in the encyclopedia?"
Pupil: (a few moments later) It says 1733.
Teacher: Is that the correct date?
Pupil: Sure it's correct, it's in the encyclopedia.
Teacher: Was there really once a George Washington?
Pupil: "That's ridiculous. If there hadn't been, how could we account for all the papers signed in his name, the stories told about him by eye witnesses, the house that was his and the clothes that were his which I've seen at his home in Mt. Vernon?"

The point of this dialogue is that children such as this one can be induced to come up with evidence upon which to base their belief in the existence of an historical figure like George Washington, or in historical events. They are compelled to get an insight into the nature of history. They see what would be necessary to account for if the belief in George Washington's existence were alleged to be false. Thus, by means of a seemingly outrageous question, the teacher has moved the student from a spectator attitude toward history to a personal understanding of how to account for certain historical facts or incidents. It is this movement from spectator to participant that enables the child to take a more active role in the process of inquiry itself.

Now it is not easy to know what questions to ask when, and how to ask the right question. Moreover, it is not enough to have a few questions at hand in one's repertoire; it is equally important that they be asked in a sequence that moves the discussion towards a culmination.

In our Instructional Manuals, we provide numerous discussion plans which enable the teacher to lead the discussion strategically without having to wonder constantly what to say next. These discussion plans usually revolve around one of the leading ideas in the chapter and are so designed as to get the children to explore the concept in depth and to relate it to their personal experiences.

c. *Answering*

The questioning teacher, by his example, encourages children to question, but this does not preclude encouraging children to find answers. An answer is a stage of satisfaction in the process of inquiry; it is a plateau at which we are content to pause for a time in the course of our efforts to understand. Questioning and finding answers are among the rhythms of living, like working and resting, or like a bird perching for a while before it goes off on another flight. The answer a child arrives at may not be correct, but it is a resolution, even if only temporary, of the period of perplexity and uncertitude he or she has been experiencing.

There is seldom justification for a teacher's actively discouraging a child from finding answers. What is more important is that children be helped to develop an openness and flexibility such that they are eager to substitute effective answers for those that no longer work. In this sense, answers are beliefs. As long as our beliefs are effective in dealing with the problems that we face in life, there is no reason for us to give them up. Even when children are exposed to conflicting evidence, there exists no urgent reason for them to give up their beliefs, although it may be time they started looking around for a more sufficient explanation.

Suppose a teacher says to a child: "The trouble is that you don't have your facts straight." The child answers "Where do I get them?" One classmate answers: "Go out and look around." But another classmate answers: "Look them up in the encyclopedia." Now obviously a question has arisen as to what *facts* are. The teacher's role in such a discussion will be to encourage, by further questioning and clarification, the children's carrying the analysis as far as they possibly can.

Very often, however, where definitions are concerned, there may be no final answer. What is the universe? What is time? What is space? What is light? The question, "What is a fact?" is a question of this sort. It can be answered by a definition — but that definition will be opposed by a contrasting definition, and so on. The resolution children arrive at, incomplete as it may be from the teacher's perspective, should be respected and let stand for the time being. There will be time to come back at a later date and go over the problem again. While no belief need be final, the aim of discussion and inquiry generally, is to move towards a tentative settlement by arriving at answers and beliefs that are serviceable and satisfying.

d. *Listening*

It is not easy to catch the significance of what people say to us if we have not developed the ability to be good listeners. For example, if a person in your school makes a remark about something that you know little about, it is likely that you will pay no attention to it. This is what psychologists call "selective inattention," and nowhere is it so prevalent as in our failure to hear the remarks of children.

For example, not long ago, in one of the experimental classes in philosophy for children, a 10-year-old compared the relationship of the body to the mind with the relationship between the "grapefruit and the taste of the grapefruit." Some adults might have judged a remark of this kind "cute." Others might have not noticed it at all. But for a teacher who knows something about the nature of philosophical thinking, such a remark stands out as extremely perceptive and insightful, and the child should be encouraged to elaborate it. In other words, the child who makes a remark of this kind may not appreciate the possibilities inherent in his own words unless someone encourages him to articulate and develop such ideas so as to recognize the importance of having such insights. But if the teacher doesn't hear such remarks in the first place, then the child is not confirmed in a belief in the importance and meaningfulness of his or her own thinking, with the result that insights such as these are never developed and lost. Perhaps next time such an insight occurs, it won't be expressed.

Even if a teacher has the ability to listen to what children say, there is a very human tendency to interpret their remarks in terms of the teacher's own perspective. This interpretation can be quite different from the child's intended meaning. Thus the teacher should develop the habit of encouraging children to articulate exactly what they do mean. The teacher who is a novice at encouraging philosophical thinking among children will no doubt find much of what children say perplexing and ambiguous. The beginning teacher will be unsure whether the children's comments have philosophical importance or not. This is partly due to the teacher's expectation that children's remarks are not that philosophical, partly it is due to the teacher's own uneasiness with the evident complexities, and partly it is due to the teacher's own lack of prior exposure to philosophical ideas. As teachers grow in their knowledge of philosophy and at the same time grow in their ability to attend to and listen to what their pupils are saying, the process is likely to become increasingly richer for children and teachers alike.

Teachers must also develop their ability to grasp the seemingly disconnected or fragmentary remarks of children as part of an ongoing and developing classroom dialogue. In other words, the teacher has to have a sense that a worthwhile discussion is brewing and that the talk that is underway is promising and likely to make progress with the right kind of guidance. It is only after the teacher has had considerable experience in guiding discussions that this capacity to surmise where a verbal interchange may lead is likely to develop.

e. *Non-verbal teacher-student communication*

Obviously, a teacher does not have to wait for children to express their wondering verbally. Their faces reveal it and their conduct reveals it. Many times what is expressed by a frown, or raised eyebrows, or quizzical expression is the equivalent of the question, "Why?" or a fully developed demand for reasons. The teacher must recognize that verbal language is not the only language in which children communicate: there is also the language of gesture, the language of facial expression, the language of posture and the language of conduct. At the same time, of course, the teacher must realize that children in the class will pounce upon every one of the teacher's gestures and facial expressions in an effort to discover its meaning. Therefore, there is a non-verbal side to communication which a teacher of philosophy must take into account no less than any other teacher.

One reason for the importance of the non-verbal element in communication is that it can in many cases be inconsistent with the verbal aspects of one's language. The mother who addresses her child in endearing terms but conveys by her gestures that she would not like the child to get too close is behaving very ambiguously. We all know cases when a person says "yes" and it is obvious that they mean "no," as well as when they say "no" and it is obvious that they mean "yes." The teacher has to learn not to emanate inconsistency. Very often children may stare non-committally at you when you are talking and yet you know that they know what you mean. Or children may say that they understand, but you can see from their faces that they don't.

Although you as the teacher should try to make your non-verbal language and your verbal language consistent, you should also be conscious that children themselves are often inconsistent in what they say and what they mean, and you should try to encourage them to express exactly what they do mean, at least insofar as a learning situation is concerned. Yet communication has many purposes, and it operates on many different levels. There is no reason to eliminate its richness except where confusion or ambiguity might cause the child some harm, or cause him to be embarrassed or feel used. Sometimes, for example, adults tease a child by saying something that is interpreted on one level by the child and on another by the adults present. The adults then have a good laugh, but at the expense of the child, who isn't sure why they are laughing but suspects it is at his or her expense.

If all goes well, children will in time come to be able to read the character of the situations in which they find themselves. This will probably involve their being able to read faces, read conduct and read the nuances of situations themselves. The teacher should be able to set an example of someone who does not have to wait for children to express themselves to be able to sense the emotional tone of a classroom. Such a teacher is more likely to evoke the trust of pupils than a teacher who is indifferent to children's unverbalized but nevertheless manifest needs. Ideally, the teacher would then encourage the children in the class to pay attention and ultimately to learn to understand one another's suggested as well as manifest intentions.

f. *The Teacher as the Child's Model*

We often underestimate how important consistency is to children themselves. Very often the child looks for adults to do what they promise to do and to be what they claim people should be. It can be very demoralizing to children to discover that the adults they have taken as models may be consistent in their words but not in their lives. The adult as ethical model must be a model of integrity.

Children look for models that they can trust and have confidence in. But a model who is merely consistent is not sufficient to provide the adult guidance which children require. A model must be capable of giving children the benefit of adult experience when they need it. The slovenly teacher is one who never objects when children fail to make needed distinctions, or when they fail to group things that belong together. This can be an unfortunate influence on children, for it is only by teachers showing the importance of distinctions and correct groupings, and by manifesting a love for such distinctions in their everyday behavior that they can get children to do likewise. The teacher who hears a small child say: "Last night, I had potatoes and vegetables for dinner" or "There are Chevrolets and cars on the parkway" without questioning such groupings is failing in one of the major responsibilities of teaching. On the other hand, the teacher who sets an example of one who does make such distinctions is giving the child a model of intellectual scrupulousness which can very well have lifelong significance.

Another sense in which the teacher can serve as a model stems from the teacher's readiness to respond to the child's ideas and to communicate that such ideas are to be taken seriously. The first problem is to detect an idea as being an idea rather than just ignoring it as a somewhat unconventional way of expressing oneself. But merely to spot the idea is not enough. The teacher has got to be able to help develop it. Very often children are unable to do more than simply enunciate an insight. From there on they need help in elaborating and articulating ideas of which they may have had only a glimpse.

A teacher has got to be able to have a certain spirit of playfulness, and should realize that the development of ideas involves a kind of free construction of meanings, just as the child's playing with blocks is a free construction of form. One should not soberly press for immediate usefulness for such creative projects.

Another characteristic which can make you an important model for the child is the fairness which you exhibit towards the different ideas that are expressed in the class, as well as your fairness in dealing with each child as a person. Your concern to develop the philosophical ability of your pupils has got to be openminded. But this can be a delicate business. First of all, there are times when you may disapprove of a child's idea because you feel sure it is wrong, but you want to be careful not to give the child an impression that in rejecting the child's idea you are rejecting the child himself. On another occasion you may feel that an idea voiced by one of the students is incorrect, yet you prefer to keep silent in the hope that the classroom dialogue will gradually demonstrate to children the reasons why their ideas are unsound.

There may be times when you disagree with an idea which has been voiced and when the reasons opposing it as offered by members of the class seem to you insufficiently convincing. You may choose to voice your own opinion, but make it clear to the class that it is simply another opinion to be considered in the light of the whole discussion. Obviously, you should not take the latter alternative unless you are sure that the class is mature enough to accept your idea as just another view and handle it on an equal footing with the views expressed by the class members.

Chapter Six

GUIDING

A PHILOSOPHICAL

DISCUSSION

1. PHILOSOPHY AND THE STRATEGIES OF DIALOGUE

Philosophy is a discipline that considers alternative ways of acting, creating and speaking. To discover these alternatives, philosophers persistently appraise and examine their own assumptions and presuppositions, question what other people normally take for granted, and speculate imaginatively concerning ever more comprehensive frames of reference. These activities in which philosophers engage are the outgrowth of philosophical training. Philosophical education is most successful when it encourages and enables people to engage in critical questioning and inventive reflection. Given this philosophical conduct as our educational objective, our immediate problem is this: what teaching methodology will ensure the production of the finest ideas and the most relevant and sustained questioning from students?

Conditions which satisfy these requirements include a teacher who is provocative, inquisitive, impatient of mental slovenliness, and a classroom of students eager to engage in dialogue that challenges them to think and produce ideas. The minimal constituents of an adequate environment in which to encourage a child to think philosophically are a questioning teacher and a group of students prepared to discuss those things that really matter to them.

Built into the very nature of philosophy is the methodology by which it is best taught — questioning and discussion. The methodology of encouraging children to think philosophically is exhibited in the discovery approach exemplified by *Harry Stottlemeier's Discovery* and *Lisa*. The teacher is an authority figure primarily in the sense of being the arbiter of the discussion process. But in addition to being a referee, the teacher should be viewed as a facilitator whose task is to stimulate children to reason about their own problems through classroom discussions.

It would be very unfortunate if the teacher in this program were to feel that there is a specific amount of content which must be covered every day, which must be extracted from each episode and eventually mastered by the students. On the contrary, a successful class is usually one in which students enter into an animated discussion that deals with something or other in the book, although the conversation may range far afield from the initial topic. Such discussions are capable of creating lasting impressions on children.

The amount of information or knowledge children acquire is less essential to their philosophical education than the development of their intellectual judgment. It is less important that children remember certain data than that they learn to think effectively. It is here that "every difference makes a difference." That is, any difference, no matter how slight, in children's modes of thinking, can conceivably modify their entire thought process. For example, a child may, until this year, have been operating on the assumption that things are pretty much what they seem to be, and suddenly he or she discovers that some things are quite different from what they seem to be. The discovery that looks can be deceiving is capable of changing that child's whole life.

Since the stress in the philosophy for children program is on the *process* of discussion, and is not aimed at achieving one specific conclusion, you do not need to present yourself to your students as possessing a great store of information. It is better for you to appear to the class as a questioner who is interested in stimulating and facilitating the discussion. You need not claim to be infallibly right or wrong. But you may very well express interest in differences among points of view, or in confirmations or contradictions of particular opinions. It has been observed that in such an atmosphere of intellectual give-and-take, students hitherto withdrawn or reserved begin to put forth their opinions because they realize that, in such an atmosphere, each point of view will be respected and taken seriously. Such children are willing to take their chances with the ensuing discussion, and to develop reasons for their opinions.

Although one doesn't *teach* philosophical topics to children, it is possible to elicit from them the wondering and questioning characteristic of philosophical behavior at any age. Gradually the children in the classroom begin to discover that a philosophical discussion has a different style from any other type of discussion. It's not just a matter of getting things off their chests, or being able to indulge in self-expression. They begin to realize that they are able to compare notes, experiences and perspectives with one another. Gradually they perceive pieces beginning to fit together into an objective picture of the way things might be. They begin to understand the importance of recognizing other people's point of view, and of giving reasons for their own opinions. There emerges a sense of the value of impartiality, and a need to think problems through rather than be satisfied with superficial or glib expressions of opinion.

Although philosophy for children may include some rigorous aspects such as the rules and principles of logic, you need not be perturbed if the discussion goes off in any meaningful direction the children care to take it, although, of course, you should always exercise judgment as to the relevance of the discussion and as to whether the length of time devoted to any particular discussion is or is not disproportionate. Moreover, there is a big difference between a "bull session" and a philosophical discussion. A philosophical discussion is cumulative; it grows or develops, and through it the participants may discover endlessly new horizons. The art of the teacher here consists in skillfully eliciting comments from the children in such a way as to keep the discussion building, while yet involving the greatest possible participation from the class. Your role throughout the discussion is one of a talented questioner. With an eye to encouraging convergent (and sometimes divergent) lines of discussion, with a recognition that a dialogue is often open-ended and somewhat unstructured, you will recognize opportunities for the children to explore new vistas, just as there will be opportunities to indicate how ideas can fit together and reinforce each other.

Under suitable circumstances, a room full of children will pounce on an idea in the way a litter of kittens will pounce on a ball of yarn thrown in their direction. The children will kick the idea around until it has been developed, elaborated upon, and even in some instances applied to life situations, although this latter is seldom achieved without the teacher's artful guidance. Yet, when the discussion is finished, they may make such remarks as "time to get back to our school work," as if what they had been doing all along was not school, or learning, or discovery of their own intellectual prowess. They may take philosophy to be nothing more than fun and games, not realizing that it may be as intellectually formative as anything they might encounter in their school experience.

2. GUIDING A CLASSROOM DISCUSSION

A thoughtful discussion is no easy achievement. It takes practice. It requires the development of habits of listening and reflecting. It means that those who express themselves during a discussion must try to organize their thoughts so as not to ramble on pointlessly. Very young children may either wish to talk all at once or not talk at all. It takes time for them to learn sequential procedures that a good discussion requires.

One of the reasons that the process of discussion is so difficult for children to learn is that they are so frequently lacking in models of good discussion with which they can identify. If neither the home nor the school offers them examples of thoughtful discussion — whether of adults with children, or even of adults with adults — then each generation of children must in effect invent the whole process of discussion by itself, because no one ever shows it how. In short, it is useful to have an established tradition of discussion which each child can automatically assimilate and identify with and engage in if dialogue is to enter meaningfully into the educational process.

One of the merits of *Harry Stottlemeier's Discovery* and *Lisa* is that they offer models of dialogue, both of children with one another, and of children with adults. They are models that are non-authoritarian, anti-indoctrinational, that respect the values of inquiry and reasoning, encourage the development of alternative modes of thought and imagination, and sketch out what it might be like to live and participate in a small commuity where children have their own interests yet respect each other as people, and are capable at times of engaging in cooperative inquiry for no other reason than that it is satisfying to do so.

Perhaps one of the most distinctive features of *Harry* and *Lisa* is that they suggest how children are able to learn from one another. This is a problem that is encountered today at every level of education: there are students in colleges, secondary schools and elementary schools who try to "make it on their own" without really seeking to learn from one another or to assimilate the life experience of their peers even when, through discussion, it might be readily available to them.

While some children speak up readily enough but fail to listen to one another, others listen intently, follow the line of the discussion and may then respond to it by making a contribution which goes beyond, rather than merely repeats, what has been said. The teacher should, of course, be aware of the possibility that the child who doesn't always listen may be developing a very unusual set of ideas, and needs to disregard the conversation for a while in order to do so. (The harm some children do to themselves by not listening is therefore likely to be considerably less than the harm other children do to themselves when, having failed to listen, they are constantly forced to cover the same ground that others have already gone over.) On the other hand, there are children who seldom speak up, but who listen intently and constructively to the class discussion. They are alert and involved, even though they fail to join in the discussion.

A discussion should build by way of its own dynamics. Like children in a playground building a pyramid by standing on one another, a discussion builds upon the contributions of each of its members. In asking questions, the teacher is not merely trying to elicit answers already known. Encouraging philosophical thinking is a matter of getting children to reflect in fresh ways, to consider alternative methods of thinking and acting, to deliberate creatively and imaginatively. The teacher cannot possibly know in advance the answers that children are going to come up with. In fact, it is just this element of surprise which has always been so refreshing about teaching philosophical thinking: one never is quite sure what thought will surface next.

It is, of course, important to keep the discussion going. As the children hear about each other's experiences and begin to learn from each other, they begin to appreciate one another's point of view and to respect one another's values. But when it appears that the discussion of one of the leading ideas of the episodes has ceased to be productive, the teacher must be prepared to direct the discussion tactfully to another topic.

3. THE ROLE OF IDEAS IN A PHILOSOPHICAL DIALOGUE

It is not unlikely that you have been wondering for some time what is distinctive about a philosophical discussion. In what ways may a philosophical discussion be contrasted with other kinds of discussions? Here we may distinguish philosophical discussion from discussions of two other types: scientific and religious.

a. *Scientific Discussions*

A scientific discussion is generally concerned with matters of fact, and with theories about matters of fact. The questions raised in a scientific discussion are in principle answerable questions. They can be answered by discovering relevant evidence, or by consulting acknowledged scientific authorities, or by making appropriate observations, or by citing pertinent laws of nature, or by conducting relevant experiments. Discussions in a science class can be very intense and very lively, especially if there is some disagreement as to how certain evidence is to be interpreted, or as to whether a given theory explains all the relevant factual data.

By and large, the scientist is dealing with how some portion of the world is to be described and explained. Therefore, a science class may involve discussion of such questions as what are the causes of sun spots, what is the temperature of dry ice, how does the heart work, how does the blood circulate, what was the Stone Age, what causes earthquakes, and so on. In general, the issues raised by these questions can be clarified and grasped by adequate discussion and analysis of elementary scientific theories and available scientific evidence. So a scientific discussion is subject to the authority of empirical evidence, as such evidence is interpreted within the accepted framework of scientific understanding. In principle, therefore, the resolution of scientific disputes is always possible.

b. *Discussions About Religious Beliefs*

Many children in your class are already in possession of a set of religious beliefs acquired from their parents, from their religious schools, from discussion with their peers, and sometimes from their own observations. These beliefs may relate to the purpose or destiny of the world, the question of personal immortality, the existence of a God, the expectation of divine reward or punishment, and so on. These are not generally the sort of questions that can be decided by factual evidence one way or another. In no way is it part of your role as a philosophy teacher to criticize a child's religious beliefs, or to seek to undermine them even in an indirect fashion. The teacher simply cannot infringe upon the realm of children's religious beliefs without becoming guilty of indoctrination. On the other hand, there can be no serious objection to affording the child a view of the range of alternatives from which human beings throughout the world select their beliefs. After all, if it is not indoctrination to suggest to children who profess to believe in many gods, or in none at all, that there are conceivable alternatives to their views, why should it not also be possible to suggest to those who believe in a solitary supernatural being that there are many numerical alternatives?

It is always unfortunate when a teacher, out of self-righteousness or ignorance, attempts to modify the religious beliefs of children in the classroom. Such invasion of the child's intellectual integrity represents not only a lack of respect for the child but also a misconception on the teacher's part of the nature of science, the nature of philosophy, and the nature of education. Some individuals think that children's religious beliefs are unsound in light of what we know of science and philosophy, and can be corrected with a healthy dash of scientific or philosophical information. But there are no such facts that can dispel religious beliefs one way or another. To the extent that religious beliefs are matters of faith, it is a question whether they are matters which can be resolved by either science or philosophy.

It is, of course, quite possible for children to have religious discussions, just as they may discuss their families, their friends, their fears, their joys and other private matters among themselves. An informal religious discussion among children typically involves a comparing and contrasting of their respective feelings and thoughts about religious matters. It does not usually involve the search for *underlying assumptions*, or the analysis of the meaning of concepts, or the search for clear definitions which often characterize philosophical discussions. In other words, religious discussions usually do not explore the assumptions on which religious beliefs rest, while a philosophical discussion cannot rest content unless it does explore its own assumptions.

To repeat, you must be very careful that this course in philosophical thinking does not serve as a tool in your hands or in the hands of the students to disparage the religious beliefs of some of the children in your class. The course optimally should serve as a tool by means of which children can clarify and find firmer foundations *for their own beliefs.* Your role is twofold. It is not to change children's beliefs but to help them find better and more sufficient reasons for believing those things *they* choose, upon reflection, to believe in. And further, your role is to strengthen their understanding of the issues involved in their holding to the beliefs they do hold.

c. *Philosophical Discussion*

We have tried to show that science and religion represent very separate areas of human interest in terms of their relevance to the classroom. In other words, from an educational point of view, scientific discussions and religious discussions are separate things and should not be confused with philosophical discussions.

Philosophical discussions need not just take up where science and religion leave off. Philosophical discussions can frequently become involved in questions of science and questions of religion, as philosophical discussions may lead into any other subject. Philosophy may or may not be a party to the dispute over factual descriptions of the world or religious interpretation of reality. As an objective onlooker, a philosopher is no more party to these disputes than an umpire is one of the contestants in a game which he referees. If anything, the umpire represents the spirit of impartiality which tries to see that the game proceeds in the fairest possible fashion. In a somewhat similar fashion, philosophy is concerned to clarify meanings, uncover assumptions and presuppositions, analyze concepts, consider the validity of reasoning processes, and investigate the implications of ideas and the consequences in human life of holding certain ideas rather than others.

This is not to imply that philosophy is concerned only with the clarification of concepts: it is also a fertile source of new ideas. For wherever there is a threshold of human knowledge, those who think about that particular subject area can only grope and cast about speculatively in an effort to understand what is there. Gradually, as methods of investigation of the new subject area are developed, as methods of observation and measurement and prediction and control are perfected, the period of philosophical speculation is replaced by one of scientific understanding. In this sense, philosophy is the mother of all sciences, for as philosophical speculation becomes more rigorous and substantiated, as measurement and experimentation and verification begin to occur, philosophy turns into science. In this sense, philosophy is a source of ideas that precedes the development of every new scientific enterprise.

Now what does all of this mean for the role of the teacher in guiding *philosophical* discussions? First, the teacher has got to keep in mind the distinctions just made between scientific, religious and philosophical discussions and must retain these subtle distinctions as guideposts in encouraging children to think philosophically. The teacher must be aware that what began as a philosophical discussion can easily turn into a dispute over factual information which can be settled only by looking up the empirical evidence that is available. It is the teacher's role, once the discussion has taken this turn, to suggest where the empirical evidence may be found, rather than continue along speculative lines. For example, it is not a philosophical dispute if an argument develops in a classroom over the sum of 252 and 323. It *is*, however, a philosophical question to ask, "what is addition?", or "what is a set?" It is easy enough to look up in a book the exact year when Columbus landed in the Western Hemisphere. However, this in no way settles the question of "who was the first person to discover the Western Hemisphere?", a notion which is very rich in ambiguity and in need of clarification. We assume that it takes *time* for light to reach the earth from the sun. But we do not have a science of time itself, and therefore, when children ask "what is time?", they are asking a philosophical question, and there is no reason why, through dialogue with their peers and teachers, they should not be exposed to some of the alternative views that have been offered by philosophers if these views can be phrased in terms that they can understand.

Philosophical discussions can evolve out of a great many of the demands children make for the *meaning* of an idea. It is up to the teacher to seize upon these opportunities and use them as entries into philosophical exploration. If the child wants to know what the word 'authority' means, or what the word 'culture' means, or what the word 'world' means, or what the word 'respect' means, or what the word 'rights' means, the teacher can take any of these as a starting point for getting as many views out on the table as there are children in the classroom, exposing the children to additional views that have been thought up by philosophers, examining the consequences of holding one view over another, and clarifying the meaning and the underlying assumptions of each view.

d. How is Philosophy Related to Science Education?

It is sometimes pointed out that scientific 'facts' are often presented in the classroom as if they were final and absolute. Such an approach is contrary to the spirit of scientific inquiry, for which no fact can ever be called indubitable. To deny the student the right to doubt the outcome of a scientific inquiry is to forestall the continuation of that inquiry. On the other hand, what the instructor needs always to make clear is that the 'facts' which he teaches rest upon evidence which is always retrievable or in some fashion demonstrable. It is only when science is taught in such a way as to ignore the limitations of empirical procedures that it becomes indoctrination.

Therefore, the benefit to scientific education of philosophy for children is that it encourages the critical temper of mind which all scientists rightly prize. When students question the facts that they are given in science, their behavior is totally in keeping with the spirit of the scientific enterprise. Indeed the philosophical frame of mind is essential as an antidote to scientific dogmatism, and as a source of fresh and provocative new ideas to be followed up by scientific investigations.

Many of the difficulties experienced by present-day programs in science education are due to to the fact not many young people appreciate what science is about. They find little in it to identify with; they do not understand the methodology; they have little sense of the difference between accurate and inaccurate ways of reasoning, nor do they have a general sense of the purpose of understanding things scientifically. It is difficult to see how students who have not been trained to value the difference between efficient reasoning and sloppy reasoning can function effectively with scientific materials. It is hard to see how students who have not been trained to draw proper inferences from what they perceive or from verbal formulations can ever be trained to engage in scientific experimentation.

In brief, we are suggesting that approaches to science education which should provide the student with a preliminary orientation toward the scientific enterprise itself, should provide incentives that would motivate children to apply themselves to scientific pursuits, and should provide a set of working habits which would combine their creative and imaginative inclinations with their own desire to think in a disciplined and orderly way about the world. Putting philosophy in the curriculum could be a step in the direction of the achievement of these goals.

The questioning inherent to philosophy is a necessary precondition to the success of a course in science; if postponed until after instruction in science is well underway, it is often too late to maintain the high level of curiosity which successful scientific education must preserve. Philosophy for children, dealing as it does with so many of the questions which children naturally have about their own life experiences, creates conditions under which the scientific instruction they receive will continue to be relevant for them. Frequently it is the lack of such connections that endangers a more traditionally presented program. It is our thesis that philosophy can provide this continuity, and that science can be more effectively taught, in terms of the objectives of science educators themselves, when a philosophy for children program is present than when it is absent.

4. FOSTERING PHILOSOPHICAL DIALOGUE

a. Discussions, Good Discussions, and Philosophical Discussions

Now and then, one will hear this sort of comment during a lunch-hour conversation among teachers: "We had a good discussion in class today." Such a remark leaves one with the impression that good discussions don't happen very often. It's something like hearing the remark, "My Uncle Fud was sober last week": One is left with the impression that the weeks Uncle Fud isn't drunk are few and far between.

But we tend to think of good discussions as pretty much a matter of luck. We're grateful for the good fortune which brings us a delightful classroom dialogue as we're grateful for a pleasant day in February—but we assume that we could no more promote the one than the other.

Yet this is a decided mistake. Good discussions can definitely be promoted—and so can good *philosophical* discussions. But first we must know just what it is we're trying to achieve. We must know how to distinguish mere discussions from good discussions, and must know what is distinctive about philosophical discussions.

One can have good discussions on any topic—in contrast to discussions that are aimless or superficial. A good discussion need not involve everyone present (some people learn more by listening than by talking; some people are thoroughly involved participants, even though silent). A good discussion does not necessarily take place just because many participants are engaged in verbalization. Nor can one contentedly lay claim to having had a good discussion just because the class has been polarized, or because a few participants have squared off against one another.

A good discussion occurs in any subject when the net result or outcome of the discussion is discerned as marking a definite progress as contrasted with the conditions which existed when the episode began. Perhaps it is a progress in understanding; perhaps it is progress in arriving at some kind of consensus; perhaps it is progress only in the sense of formulating the problem—but in any case, there is a sense of forward movement having taken place. Something has been accomplished: a group product has been achieved.[1]

In contrast, a mere discussion may evoke comments from various individuals present (one hesitates to call them "participants,") but without achieving a "meeting of minds." Individuals may succeed in expressing the perspectives from which they perceive the issue, but the perspectives never intersect so as to form parts of some larger frame of reference. A series of individuals may testify as to their beliefs, but they could just as well occupy independent universes for all the connection their testimonies have with one another.

Yet a mere discussion may be the soil out of which a good discussion springs, as a good discussion on any topic may be the soil out of which a philosophical discussion springs. The point is that we can tell what is good about a good discussion by what *emerges* as the discussion proceeds. A mere discussion is linear and episodic, like a mediocre picaresque novel in which a series of incidents is strung together, yet nothing ever *builds*. On the other hand, a good discussion is cumulative; each contribution is in effect a line of force or vector which converges upon the others and is orchestrated with the others. Whether there is complete agreement or disagreement at the close of the episode is relatively unimportant; what matters is that the contributions from each participant relate to and reinforce one another, as each participant learns from what the others have said (and indeed, learns from his or her own contributions), and as each successive contribution to the discussion reflects the successive increments of understanding which that participant has amassed.

If one listens carefully to the remarks of the leader of a "brainstorming" session—or of the moderator at an ordinary discussion—and then compares these with the questions or comments of a teacher of philosophy, one cannot help being struck by the difference. The person whose only aim is to extract comments or opinions from as many people as possible will often address questions such as these to the participants:

---

[1] See Justus Buchler, "What is a Discussion?" *Journal of General Education*, Vol. VIII, No. 1, Oct. 1954, pp. 7-17.

What is your opinion on this matter?
What are your beliefs on this topic?
Do you agree with what has just been said?

In other words, questions such as those just mentioned merely seek to elicit opinions, but they do not promote reasoning. Each protagonist is not encouraged to formulate his views rationally, but to spew them forth, as it were, off the top of his head.

In a philosophical discussion, on the other hand, the teacher will be found asking questions such as these:

What reasons do you have for saying that?
Why do you agree (or disagree) on that point?
How are you defining the term you just used?
What do you mean by that expression?
Is what you are saying now consistent with what you said before?
Could you clarify that remark?
When you say that, just what is implied by your remarks?
What follows from what you said?
Is it possible you and he are contradicting each other?
Are you sure you're not contradicting yourself?
What alternatives are there to such a formulation?

To lead a philosophical discussion, one has to develop a feeling for which sort of question is appropriate to each situation, and for the sequences in which such questions can be asked. A teacher of philosophy may pause over a certain student's comment, pursue it, explore it, while judging that the next student's comment should be allowed to stand on its own merits without further examination, because right then further analysis might be counter-productive. No recipe can be written for the perfect discussion technique, although teachers interested in finding models could do worse than read the *Dialogues* of Plato, where Socrates is portrayed as a master teacher of philosophy—that is, the master in the art of eliciting productive dialogue.

b. Drawing Students Out

Getting students to engage in philosophical dialogue is an art. As with any art, some knowledge is a pre-requisite—in this case, the teacher should possess an understanding of when it is appropriate to intervene in the discussion and when not to. There are times when the best thing one can do to guide a discussion is to say nothing and let things happen. In fact, the goal towards which a philosophical discussion should move is one in which there is maximum *student-student* interchange, as opposed to the start of such a discussion, in which *teacher-student* interchange is at a maximum.

1. ELICITING VIEWS OR OPINIONS

We have repeatedly stressed the point that classroom discussion should begin with the interests of the students, and that having children read a story is a way of creating an experience which will mobilize and crystallize their interests. We are all familiar with the fact that our own interests tend to flag unless stimulated and directed; what is pedagogically useful in the work of art is that it animates those interests of ours which would otherwise lie dormant and inert.

Once the children have read the story, you may ask them what they found interesting in it, and as these comments are offered by the class, you may find it helpful to write them on the blackboard and check with students on accuracy of written representations of their ideas. This series of "points of interest" then becomes the agenda for the class discussion. (Note that it is essentially the children's agenda, not yours—although you may find it advantageous to add to it if the pupils seem to have overlooked something you think important.)

Now the first item on the discussion agenda is taken up. You may ask for an expression of views. If such views are slow in being offered, you may ask the person who suggested the item to elaborate on it, by asking such questions as:

> Why did you find that particular incident interesting?
> Are you familiar with incidents of this sort?
> Which views do you agree with and which do you disagree with?
> How did this part of the story help you understand the rest of it?
> Is there anything about this episode you found puzzling?
> Does this episode raise issues you think we ought to discuss?

Of course, you will probably discover you have numerous questions to ask that are much more specific and relevant to the suggested item than the rather general questions listed above. In that case, don't hesitate to begin by asking those questions which are most immediately pertinent to the agenda item under discussion.

2. HELPING STUDENTS EXPRESS THEMSELVES: CLARIFICATION AND RESTATEMENT

Sometimes, in the course of teaching your class, you may find that students have difficulty expressing themselves. Maybe they just can't find the right words; maybe they're shy. In any case you may want, on such occasions, to try to evoke student participation by means of helping phrases such as the following:

> You appear to be saying. . .
> Could it be that. . .
> Are you saying that. . .
> This is what I think I hear you saying. . .

I get the impression that. . .
Could this be what you're saying, that. . .
As I hear you, you're saying that. . .
So as you see it. . .
Correct me if I'm wrong, but isn't this. . .
Well then, from your point of view. . .
As I understand you. . .
Am I correct in assuming you are saying that. . .
Would it be reasonable to put your position like this. . .
I wonder if what you're saying could be put this way. . .
Would it help if I expressed your views this way. . .

It will be noticed that the phrases just cited are employed by the teacher to get the student to *clarify* what the child has said. They do not ask for the reasons or the implications of the child's remark; they are simply efforts *to restate* or to get the child to *restate* certain comments that need elucidation.

No doubt it is preferable that children clarify their own views rather than that you should perform this task for them. But there are times when students are stumped as to some better way of saying what they've said, and you can help by offering to reformulate their remarks in some more comprehensible form.

The advantage to your doing this is that it expedites discussion. The danger, clearly, is that what you think is an innocent translation of the child's views into a formulation more readily understood is in fact an interpretation of the original view—an interpretation that can well be a *distortion* of what the child originally intended. We all have manipulative tendencies of which we may or may not be conscious, and one way in which these come out is in our efforts to get others to believe what we believe by the device of persuading them that what they are trying to say is precisely what we would like to hear them say. But your obligation is to help children express what they think, even though what they think may turn out not to be what you would like them to think. If you don't agree with them, there may be occasions for saying so, and for explaining why you disagree. But distorting students' views by subtle reformulation is manipulative and indoctrinational—which is another way of saying that it is inappropriate to philosophical dialogue.

3. EXPLICATING STUDENTS' VIEWS

On the other hand, you may wish to do more than simply help your students clarify their views by restatement. You may want to explore not merely what they say, but the *meanings* of what they say. There is a difference between asking a student "Are you saying that ..." and asking the same student "Are you implying that ..." It is the difference between what one asserts and how that assertion is to be interpreted.

But before discussing what is involved in interpreting your students' remarks, some attention should be given to *explication*. Explication lies between undistorted restatement and interpretation. You explicate when you select and emphasize certain features of what a student has asserted. Or you can get your students themselves to explicate what they have said. These are some of the comments that are cues for explication:

Is the point you're making that. . .
Which points in what you've said would you like to emphasize?
So you think the following points are important. . .
Can I sum up your argument as follows. . .
Could you give us a quick summary of the points you're making. . .
Here's what I take to be the gist of your remarks. . .

4. INTERPRETATION

The discussion in your classroom may now turn on the *meaning* of what someone has remarked, or on the *meaning* of a passage in what the class has read. When we unpack meanings, we're engaged in interpretation.

What you say presumably has meaning to you in your frame of reference—in your life experience. But interpretation of your remarks may differ markedly from your own interpretation of what you said. In other words, you impute one meaning to your remarks, while other persons may impute quite another.

Now, in guiding a philosophical discussion, it is quite important to be aware not only of what is being said, but of how the various members of the class interpret what is being said. There are two ways in which meanings are drawn out of what has been said: by inferring what is *logically implied,* and by inference from what is *suggested* although not logically implied.

a. Inferring logical implications

By studying logic, you can learn how to tell what can be logically inferred from given statements or groups of statements. Logic will be able to tell you, for instance, that from the statement "No dogs are reptiles," you can logically infer that no reptiles are dogs, but that you cannot logically infer from it that all dogs are vertebrates, or that no reptiles are furry.

Logic will also tell you that from two statements in the following form:

All disk jockeys are human
All humans are mortal

you can legitimately draw the inference that "All disk jockeys are mortal." Logic can tell us, in other words, what is implied by what we say, insofar as what we say can be carefully formulated and arranged to suit the rules of logic. In the course of a classroom discussion, these strict conditions often do not obtain. We can study idealized instances—like Harry, in Chapter One of *Harry Stottlemeier's Discovery,* spotting an instance of invalid deductive inference—indeed, in that chapter, he spots no less than two such instances. In real life discussions, such possibilities of strict examination for logical inference are not too frequent: don't hold your breath waiting for them to happen. Nevertheless the mastery of logic equips the reader with powerful tools for the extraction of precise meanings from what has been read.

b. Inferring what is suggested

Interpretation is a matter of finding meaning through discovering what is suggested or implied by what someone has expressed. Note that people draw *inferences,* but expressions have *implications.* The implications of an expression are its meaningful consequences: some of these meaningful consequences are logically implied, and some are simply suggested.

For example, if a member of your class says, "Oh, no, Johnnie's not your pet at all—he just gets high grades because he's so brilliant!" you would not be wrong to suspect that what has been said is ironical, and that it is being *suggested* (although it is certainly not logically implied) that Johnnie's very much your pet student.

Or if someone says, "Yesterday, Frank moved up to a front seat. Today, the whole front row moved to the back of the room," surely it is being suggested that the students in the front row moved away *because* Frank moved up front—yet nowhere is this logically implied.

There are also non-verbal inferences to be detected. Your reading of these must range from catching what is suggested by an innuendo or a slightly unusual emphasis to picking up gestures or facial expressions among the class and interpreting their meanings as responses to what has been said.

Since interpretation is a matter of drawing out what is suggested or implied, at times you can move a discussion along by suitably interpreting what has been expressed by the students to that point. Your interpretations might be introduced by phrases such as:

From what has been said, I gather that. . .

If I'm not mistaken, your position can be interpreted in this way. . .

Correct me if I'm wrong, but aren't you saying, in a nutshell, that. . .

As I read what you're saying, it seems to follow logically that. . .

Are you suggesting that. . .

Are you implying that. . .

Would I be distorting what you're suggesting if I put it this way. . .

I interpret your meaning to be as follows. . .

Couldn't your meaning be put this way. . .

Could you explain what you mean by what you just said. . .

If what you're saying is correct, wouldn't it follow that. . .

If what you're saying is correct, how can you explain the fact that. .

In view of what you've just expressed, don't you think that. . .

In view of what you've just expressed, do you think that. . .

I think what you've just said is significant or insignificant because. . .

It seems to me the implications of what you've said are far-reaching because. . .

Would you object to this interpretation of your remarks. . .

5. SEEKING CONSISTENCY

It is useful in the course of a philosophical discussion to raise questions about consistency. (By "consistency" is meant the practice of using the same term in such a way as to have the same meaning when the term is employed several times in the same context.) You may suspect that a person isn't being consistent in his presentation of his views, or you may feel that the views of several individuals in the classroom are inconsistent with one another. In either case, it would be well to explore such possibilities, using questions or comments like the following:

Earlier, when you used the word _____, didn't you use it in quite a different sense from the way you are employing it now?

Are you really disagreeing with one another—or are you saying the same thing in two different ways?

It seems to me there's a direct contradiction between those two views. . .

Just to elaborate on that view for a moment, wouldn't it be consistent to add that. . .

Of course your views are consistent; but you could still be wrong because. . .

6. REQUESTING DEFINITIONS

There are times when the terms employed in a discussion get to be more confusing than illuminating. On such occasions, it may be well to pause for a definition ... or else to abandon the troublesome terms altogether.

What happens, very often, is that the controversy among your students can be traced back to the fact that they are using the identical term, but defining it in quite different ways. Once all of you become aware of this fact, you can decide whether to try to arrive at a common definition, or to find alternative terms which would be more suitable.

Your students may be disagreeing over whether a movie was good or wasn't good, or over whether a platypus is a fish, a bird or a mammal, and so on. In simple cases, such as the latter, it is obvious that a dictionary is your best recourse. But in other cases, you will find that the most controversial words are those that are very rich in alternative meanings. Try to get at the definitions which your pupils are implicitly employing—if such a step becomes necessary—by asking such questions as:

When you use the word _____, what do you mean by it?

Can you define the word _____, which you just used?

What does the word _____, refer to?

If a thing is a _____, what are its chief features?

On the whole, you should be cautious about requesting definitions, because doing so runs the risk of sidetracking the discussion into *merely* a dispute over definitions. For example, you may be discussing the problem of war, and the dialogue is progressing nicely. Then you interject the question, "What do we mean by 'war'?" It's an excellent question—but make sure you ask it at an appropriate moment, when the students are beginning to see the difficulties involved in the word, rather than at a moment when the dialogue is going along smoothly and productively because certain meanings of the word are being taken for granted.

On the other hand, there are discussions that seem to be unable to get off the ground unless one or more of the basic terms are defined at the very beginning. For example, you may be talking about what happens in Chapter Five of *Harry Stottlemeier's Discovery,* and find that it's essential to come to some understanding or consensus about the meaning of the word "education." In such cases, you might well begin by asking for the key word or words to be defined.

7. SEARCHING FOR ASSUMPTIONS

If one of the chief characteristics of philosophical dialogue is to discover what is *implied* (what follows from) what is said, another of the chief characteristics is the search for the assumptions underlying what is said. It is typical of philosophers to look for the presuppositions upon which every question and every assertion are based—and this quest likewise characterizes philosophical discussions—especially those that are most penetrating and profound.

Exposing assumptions doesn't necessarily cause students to give up those assumptions. But it may very well cause them to rethink whatever they say that is based on such assumptions.

Very often, disclosure of what a questioner presupposes reveals why the question seems unanswerable. Surely, if someone asked you how far it is from here to never-never-land, you would reject the question on various grounds, such as that it assumes that never-never-land exists, that the distance to it is measurable, that "here" is a specific location, and so on. Or, if someone asked you whether it was warmer in the winter or in the city, you would protest that the question assumed that the winter and the city could be compared in terms of temperature. Or if a question is asked, "How will the world end?" surely it is legitimate to inquire as to why the questioner is assuming that the world will end. You can present students with a model of critical scrutiny of questions and assertions to detect what the presuppositions are, and whether any of them are unwarranted. You can ask such questions as:

Aren't you assuming that. . .

Doesn't what you say presuppose that. . .

Doesn't what you say rest on the notion that. . .

Is what you've just said based on your belief that. . .

Would you say that if you didn't also happen to believe that. . .

If a child asks you something like, "How are bears different from mammals?" he may be assuming that the mammal is just another species of animal. In such a case, you may be able to correct his faulty assumption. But in another instance, you may discover that his assumption is correct, but what he has inferred from it is wrong. For example, a small child might assert that trees never die. Suppose you ask him what that belief of his is based on, and he replies, "Only living things die." Now in this case, his presupposition is correct, but he has drawn a faulty inference from it, due to the fact that he's made another—and in this case, faulty—assumption: that trees aren't living things.

8. INDICATING FALLACIES

If you take the lead in pointing out logical fallacies when you encounter them being made during a class discussion, you'll find that the students themselves will begin to take over after a while, and will begin to correct each other in similar situations.

For example, you can point out fallacies such as these:

"I wouldn't believe anything she has to say about history. Everyone knows her grandfather served time in jail."	Fallacy of attacking the person who makes the argument rather than the argument itself.
"Sure I believe what he says about politics. After all, he's the leading hitter in the National League, isn't he?"	Fallacy of appealing to an authority when the person in question isn't an authority on that particular issue.
"I kept thinking about his pitching a no-hitter. That's why he failed to pitch the no-hitter: I jinxed him."	Jumping to conclusion—in this case, assuming that the thought must have caused what happened (the loss of the no-hitter) just because it preceded what happened.

There are, of course, many other types of fallacies in addition to these, and one of the objectives of a course in logic is to enable you to recognize a considerable number of such fallacies. If you tolerate the commission of such fallacies by your students, you not only encourage sloppy thinking, but you also fail to teach them what poor reasons are. After all, if they can't always find their *best* reasons, that's still no excuse for allowing them to get away with offering their worst.

9. REQUESTING REASONS

One of the dimensions of a philosophical discussion is the development of systematic presentations of ideas. For example, a theory is not usually a single concept, but a network of concepts. Similarly, what in philosophy is called an *argument* is a systematic presentation of ideas, in that it consists of a *conclusion* supported by one or more *reasons*.

Usually, students will put forth their beliefs or opinions without troubling to support them. You should seek to elicit from them the reasons they are prepared to give in support of such beliefs or opinions. Gradually, you will find that other students will take over this role from you, and will demand reasons from their classmates. In time, many students will develop the habit of offering opinions *only* when these can be supported by reasons.

101

A reason may or may not be formally connected to a conclusion. For example, if a student says he doesn't believe there are little green men on Mars, he may offer as his reason that there is no evidence of such beings. On the other hand, he may argue (rightly or wrongly) somewhat along these lines:

Only earth inhabitants are humans.
Martians aren't earth inhabitants.
Therefore, Martians can't be humans.

This could be put into standard form as a logical argument, so that the student's reasons would serve as *premises* to support his conclusion. This class discussion would then likely shift to the controversial first premise.

In soliciting reasons for students, your questions can be fairly explicit:

What is your reason for saying that. . .

What makes you think that. . .

On what grounds do you believe that. . .

Can you offer an argument in support of your claim that. . .

Why do you say that. . .

Why do you believe your view is correct?

What can you say in defense of your view?

Is there anything you'd like to say in order to prove your view correct?

Would you like to tell us why you think that's so?

When one offers a reason in support of an opinion, it is generally because the reason is less controversial and more acceptable than the opinion it is meant to support. In other words, we appeal to reasons because they carry plausibility. Compare these exchanges:

Q: Why do you think potassium is a mineral?
A: Because my science textbook says it is.

Q: Why do you say that you don't try to get even when someone has hurt you?
A: Because two wrongs don't make a right.

Q: Why do you think foreigners are secretive?
A: Because they always talk in languages I can't understand.

Q: Shouldn't we get rid of our national anthem because it's hard to sing?
A: I think the reasons in favor of it—that it's beautiful and unusual—outweigh the reason you've just cited against it.

Q: Why have you stopped listening to the radio while you drink?
A: Because I'm tired of hearing people talk about how excessive drinking can lead to alcoholism.

Some of the reasons cited above are fairly plausible, while others are not—or are, in any case, not more plausible than the belief they are supposed to substantiate. This is why, in soliciting reasons from students, you should try to insist upon good reasons—reasons with a high degree of plausibility.

Naturally the teacher should help students distinguish between the positions they are taking and the reasons they cite in defense of such positions. But the etiquette of dialogue further requires the teacher to assist students in formulating the best reasons they can for their positions, whatever the value the teacher may place upon such positions. Thus the teacher, rather than criticize a student's weakest reasons, would do well to help such a student formulate better ones. Thus, for example, a teacher may deplore the hunting of animals. Yet suppose that, in a discussion of Chapter One of *Lisa,* a student defends hunting on the grounds that it gives hunters an invaluable opportunity to develop shooting accuracy. Surely, in a case like this, what should be done is not spend too much time considering the weakness of such an argument, for much more is to be gained by considering what better reasons for hunting might be advanced –such as that the animals are predators, or that their overpopulation is a danger — even though one may still feel that the reasons against hunting outweigh those in favor of it.

10. ASKING STUDENTS TO SAY HOW THEY KNOW

The single question, "How do you know?" can be very useful in eliciting from students a wide range of explanations.

(a) It may bring forth reasons for assertions, because some students interpret the question as a demand for reasons.
For example:

"I think it's going to rain."
"How do you know?"
"Because the weather forecast is for rain."

(b) It may bring forth a citation of evidence for the assertion—observations or data which are offered in support of what has been stated or claimed. For example:

"I think it's going to rain."
"How do you know?"
"Well, there are those storm clouds out there to the north, the wind's beginning to rise, the barometer's dropping, and my ankle's beginning to hurt the way it always does when it's about to rain."

(c) Or, the question, "How do you know?" can bring forth explanations which deal very literally with *how one knows*. For example:

"I think it's going to rain."

"How do you know?"

"By reflecting on the evidence, and by taking into account my past experience."

Obviously, there is a difference between asking students why they believe what they believe—in effect, asking for reasons—and asking them how they know what they know. The latter is literally a request for them to explain the process of knowing, and to say why, when they feel sure they're right, they feel the way they do.

11. ELICITING AND EXAMINING ALTERNATIVES

If a student were to express the view that, in order to become rich, one ought to be dishonest, surely you would want to show him that there are alternatives — that many people have become wealthy without being dishonest and that many people have sought other goals in life than wealth. Eventually the choice would still be his, but at least you would have helped him see the options.

It is not infrequent for children to insist that the way they view things is the only possible way for such things to be viewed. They haven't considered any alternatives because they don't think there are any alternatives to consider. This is where you can liberate them from narrow-mindedness — by suggesting that there might very well be other possibilities to explore, and by helping them to identify and examine such alternative possibilities.

Thus, if a student insists that all objects must fall to earth, you might ask the members of the class if it's possible for objects not to fall to earth. If a student expresses the view that there is no such thing as personal survival after death, you might want to explore what alternative possibilities there are to that view. Likewise the student who earnestly believes that everything is wonderful (no less than the student who believes that everything is dreadful) probably needs to engage in a closer consideration of the options.

You can encourage children to realize that there are alternatives to their views by means of such comments as:

There are some people who think that ...

Would you say that any other beliefs on this subject are possible?

How else could this matter be viewed?

Does anyone else have a different view?

Suppose someone wanted to contradict your view — what position could they take?

Is your view the only one people might take on this topic?

Are there circumstances where your opinion might be incorrect?

Are there other ways of looking at this matter that might be more believable?

Are there other ways of looking at this matter which may be possible, even though false?

Is it possible that other explanations than yours are possible?
Couldn't it also be that ....?
What if someone were to suggest that ....?

It should be remembered that the purpose of opening up alternatives to children is not to confuse or bewilder them, but to liberate them from narrow-mindedness or rigidity. The purpose is not to compel them to choose other convictions than those they already have, but to equip them to discover and assess their intellectual options.

C. Orchestrating a Discussion

The suggestions offered above regarding ways of drawing students out so as to elicit and facilitate philosophical dialogue are largely tactical. That is, their value is fairly specific. As a teacher, however, you must keep more general pedagogical strategies in mind, in addition to developing a repertoire of dialectical tactics.

1. *Grouping ideas*—For example, you may find it useful to keep in mind the various suggestions students have made, and to assemble these into groups or clusters, each representing a specific position or pattern of argument. You can be very helpful to the students in your class if you can then sum up each of these positions or arguments, for you will provide a sense of proportion or perspective which your pupils might otherwise have been incapable of attaining. Obviously, if the class discussion has polarized the class so explicitly that everyone is aware of the different positions being taken, such summarization by you would likely be redundant and superfluous. So you should save it for those occasions on which it's needed.

2. *Suggesting possible lines of consequence or divergence*—As you become more adept at organizing discussions, you'll find that your motive in asking this question or that will be determined by certain strategic considerations, such as that you'd like to broaden the range of views being offered by students, or that you'd like to steer some of the strands of discussion into greater convergence with one another.

(a) To open a discussion up, and to encourage a greater divergency of views, you may find it useful to introduce distinctions at certain crucial points which allow for a sharpening of differences among members of the class. For example, in Chapter Five of *Harry,* Mark argues that all schools are bad. Harry, however, argues that only those schools are bad which are run by people who don't understand children, thereby offering a distinction that allows for more precise analysis than Mark's more sweeping claim. You could, in like manner, seek to introduce distinctions which would increase the number of options open to the children in the classroom. Also, you can introduce additional points of view into a discussion by such remarks as those just cited under the heading "Eliciting and examining alternatives."

(b) At times you may want to show that certain views which have been expressed in class are not only different, but are in direct conflict with one another. To do this, you may resort to pointing out that the two views are *incompatible* because their implications eventually contradict one another. For example, suppose one person in the class asserts that, "No girls are scouts," and another person asserts that, "Some scouts are girls." Simply using the logic in *Harry* (in other words, by reversing the subject and predicate of the first statement), you should be able to show the class that the two original statements are incompatible. because they lead to statements which are in contradiction with one another.

(c) On other occasions, you will want to take the initiative in the classroom by showing *connections* which your students would not otherwise have noted. You may want to point out that certain things they have thought to be distinct could quite reasonably be grouped together. Or you may point out that two arguments which different members of the class have advanced are really saying pretty much the same thing—or are *convergent* upon the same general position. Thus your role as a teacher may sometimes be to unify the class in spite of expressed differences, just as at other times your role may be that of encouraging children to appreciate diversity and multiplicity. You can encourage *divergence* when making distinctions where necessary. There is no sure recipe as to which approach you should emphasize, but you would probably do well to consider your position as a discussion leader to be a *remedial* one, supplying that component—whether it be unity or diversity—which the discussion has signally lacked until that point.

3. Moving discussions to higher levels of *generality*—Elsewhere in this book we have referred to the tendency of children's questions to advance a discussion to a higher level of generality. Thus a child asked to add two numbers may first want an explanation of *number,* or a child asked about the size of his house may inquire in turn what *size* is.

In *Harry* and *Lisa,* there are frequent instances in which children stop to consider the concepts and terms that we use when we reflect, rather than continue to utilize such terms and concepts unreflectively. As a teacher, you too will likely find it useful frequently to direct discussion to concepts or notions that are being taken for granted, but which are in need of analysis.

In so doing, you will probably raise the discussion to a higher level of generality. Your aim should not be to make the discussion more abstract, but to make it more comprehensive. For example, you may be discussing in class whether it is fair to define adulthood at different ages—one age for voting, another for theater admissions, etc. Or you may be discussing the policy of the mass media to accept liquor ads for magazines but not for television. And in these instances, as the discussion proceeds, you may find it useful to ask, "What is fairness?" or "What is consistency?" You will thus raise the discussion to a truly philosophical level—and you and your students will feel the profound satisfaction that can develop when you have come to grips with a subject on its highest level of generality. For it is in this way that a philosophical discussion seeks to deal with what is most fundamental in human experience.

Chapter 7

LOGIC

FOR CHILDREN

Harry and *Lisa* directly challenge long-established presumptions about the character of an introduction to philosophy, and to logic in particular. Neither is organized in a standard introductory format — they are neither "problem" nor "history" oriented. Instead, the books are constructed of a series of dialogues between children. Though adults often make contributions, the books consistently retain this child-centered perspective.

The dialogues are composed of a variety of themes, some overlapping, some confined to particular discussions. These include such diverse topics as the nature of the mind, whether the pledge to the flag should be mandatory, distinguishing between differences in degree and kind, that persons differ from things, seeing shapes in clouds, who threw a rock at Harry Stottlemeier, reasons versus causes, and the varieties of thinking. Entwined with these strands is a main theme which appears in various guises in every chapter: the development of effective ways to think about thinking. This is the key to how logic is introduced and developed in philosophy for children — never as a barren set of formulas, but always in contexts of reflective thinking, especially in efforts to think more clearly about thinking itself.

1. RULE-GOVERNED AND OTHER TYPES OF THINKING

The basic purpose of each book is to provide its readers with a means for attending to their own thoughts and to ways that their thoughts and reflections can function in their lives. This is approached through a discovery of rule-governed thinking, and by illustrations of a variety of non-formal types of thought. The logical rules are not simply stated for the reader to learn; instead, the books provide illustrations of rules and of search-techniques so that their readers can come to identify such rules of their own. This is most important — the books are designed to encourage their readers to pay careful attention to their *own* thoughts and ideas, rather than acquire significant reflections by striving to think someone else's thoughts, as is the case with even the most up to date school texts. Together with the discovery that certain kinds of thinking are rule-governed, readers are also made aware of contrasting modes of thought such as imagining, dreaming, pretending, in which logical rules play little or no part. Through coming to appreciate and enjoy this broad variety of kinds of thinking, the readers can then realize that while their thinking often has logical form and occasionally fails to when it should, much of it does not and need not.

Rule-governed thinking, in both books, is exemplified by the discovery and development of formal logic. But there is far more to reflective thinking than formal logic alone. As there are explicit rules of formal logic, so too can one speak of implicit rules of procedures, rules which bear on matters such as the pursuit of inquiry, listening to others and thinking out what they have to say, and thinking for oneself. So there are three main types of rule-related thinking exhibited in these books. There is thinking by the rules, where the rules are those of formal logic; there is thinking against the rules, where the rules of formal logic are either violated (as in the case of fallacious thinking), or ignored (as in dreams and imaginings); and there is thinking in accordance with rules, where the rules are procedural rather than formal, and consist of general guidelines as to what is and what is not reasonable.

2. TWO LOGICAL MODELS

A close look at *Harry* and *Lisa* show that they employ two distinct models of logic. One, exhibited through a progressive discovery of rules explicitly stated, is that of a deductive system of formal logic. The other consists of a kind of "good reasons" approach. In place of abstract inference patterns, this emphasizes the *seeking* of reasons for opinions, actions, and beliefs, together with the *assessment* of the reasons given. The latter never takes the form of an investigation of the formal structure of inferences, but instead depends upon an intuitive sense of what can count as a good argument. As a result, in place of the formal rules of the first model, this second logical model yields a string of exemplary arguments which have certain procedural similarities, but which do not conform to fixed deductive patterns.

In contrasting these two logical models, we do not mean to imply that the first applies only when the children talk about thinking, while the second is confined to their actual arguments. In two prominent cases in *Harry*, for instance, the discovery of a formal rule is followed by its successful application to a matter of direct concern to the children, where both these applications are recognized to be in argument form. The contrast between the models is more clearly connected to a common ambiguity in what is meant by "rule-governed thinking" than to any solid difference between actual states of affairs.

In the case of the first, formal deductive model, to say that it is a model of rule-governed thinking is to say that the rules of which it is composed are *structural*, putting specific constraints on the kinds of *inferences* permitted in terms of the *internal structure* of sentences. For example, one of the first explicit rules in *Harry* is a rule of conversion: "if a true sentence begins with the word 'no,' then its reverse is also true. But if it begins with the word 'all,' then its reverse is false." However, the second good reasons model is one of governed thinking in that it involves *normative* rules, rules that put general constraints on the sorts of *reasons* that can be put forth in support of an action or belief. For example, when one of the children supports an opinion by reference to what her father says, this is challenged by questioning whether her father is an authority on the matter under dispute: "I'm afraid that that won't do. You should only use someone else's opinion as a reason for your own view if that other person is a recognized authority on the subject in question." The criterion here does not apply to the internal structure of the reason cited, but instead appraises appeals to authority, permitting a certain kind of appeal as a good reason, disallowing others. Such criteria can of course be deductive — formal rules of inference can be used as norms for appraising reasons put forth in support of some claim. But there are other types of criteria of appraisal, such as those appropriate to inductive arguments; to arguments from analogy; to arguments justifying beliefs, or actions; to arguments from authority, etc.

While the good reasons approach provides much of the logical substance to *Harry* and *Lisa*, it is never explicitly recognized and discussed by the children in the books. Thus, all their talk about logical rules, or rules of thinking, is confined to the development of formal logic. But that very development illustrates the contrast between formal deductive and good reasons logics.

The first rule mentioned in *Harry* is discovered by accident, tried out on some examples, then modified. The source of this rule is two sentences that happen to suggest it, but the other rules are acquired in a variety of ways, including seeing an analogy, asking help from other members of a class (including the teacher), consulting a teacher directly, thinking out logical alternatives, shared inquiry among two children, something learned from a cousin who teaches high school math, and generalizing from instances. Rules are modified in some cases by discovery of counter-instances, in others by a teacher who combines a plurality of rules into one general rule. Most stated rules are subsequently illustrated by examples, but no specific technique is advocated for testing them; in some cases they are treated as generalizations to be tested against individual cases, in others they are simply accepted, for example, as when devolving from an authority. With the exception of the use of counterinstances, none of these search and testing procedures conform to deductive formal reasoning. But in their uses of analogies, inductive generalizations, authorities, and suchlike, they do rely on the sorts of normative rules characteristic of the good reasons model.

In trying to understand the significance of the rules they discover, the children in *Harry* sometimes interpret the rules in terms of mathematical sets or classes. A diagram of two concentric circles is used to illustrate the reason why conversions (reversals) of sentences beginning with "all" turn true sentences into false ones, and certain patterns of formal inference are explained by saying that the word "are" really means "belong to the class of." But the children also question formal logic by discussing whether it is worthwhile to try to discover and master such rules. This theme appears early in *Harry*, echoes through several chapters, and reaches a crescendo in the final, seventeenth chapter. There they decide (a) that they should try to see things from other people's points of view, (b) that some people think in patterns which conform to the rules, hence (c) in order to see things as those people do, they need to get to know the rules. The key to shared access to these rules is then said to be that they "work with the way we talk."

Clearly, these considerations belong to the good reasons model. The main theme, to try to see things from other persons' points of view, is a rich metaphor which ranges in interpretation from literally seeing physical objects from a variety of physical perspectives to developing an empathic understanding of the thoughts and feelings of other persons. But it is just this ambiguity which prevents using the main theme in any formal deductive sense as support for learning the rules. As a metaphor, talk about seeing things from the viewpoints of others does supply a reason for studying formal logic — insofar as the rules of formal logic do apply to the ways we talk, they provide criteria for assessing discussions which can lead to understanding the views of others, though whether this is a *good* reason or not is left for the readers of *Harry* to decide.

3. MENTAL ACTS AND STYLES OF THOUGHT

Among the main themes of both books, sharply reiterated in the arguments in the closing chapters of *Harry*, is the view that only some people think in patterns conforming to the rules of formal logic, and that such rules are appropriate to only certain types of thinking. Both books present, in explicit contrast, a broad variety of other sorts of thinking. This plurality of styles of thinking is exhibited in two criss-crossing ways. First, the individual children each display a predominant style of thought. Second, each child eventually uses more than this one style. Thus, while one type dominates for each child, what is characteristic of one is also exhibited — less often, though occasionally — by others. The result is a complex matrix of types of thinking, such that for certain strands the developing formal logic is appropriate, for others obviously not so, while the rest provide a gray area to which good reasons logic often applies. This is all sufficiently complicated, and close to the philosophic core of logic for children, to warrant detailed attention.

A survey of *Harry*, for example, shows that there are at least 86 different kinds of mental acts attributed to the children in the book. These range from being suddenly aware that one is being looked at, to sharing a special insight with a friend, from wondering whether one's grandfather will keep a promise to buy a football to constructing a rule of formal logic. Those most commonly displayed (used by the same child in at least five different situations) include thinking something to oneself, thinking about oneself, remembering, being uncertain, drawing an inference (using a rule of formal logic), consciously expressing an opinion, devising an example for a proposed rule, trying to figure something out, wondering (whether, why, how, what), and making a decision.

Among the major characters, certain kinds of mental acts, especially logical ones, recur. These predispositions to think in certain ways constitute differing styles of thinking; one such style is deductive, others include variants of the good reasons approach. Those which predominate are wondering (Harry Stottlemeier), thinking in formal logical patterns (Tony Melillo), intuitive or hunch-like thinking (Lisa Terry), seeking and enjoying explanations (Fran Wood), being sensitive to the feelings of others (Anne Torgerson), and thinking independently (Mickey Minkowski). While this is only a partial list of types of mental acts and associated styles of thinking illustrated in *Harry*, one can already see that they constitute a very broad network. Mental acts and styles of thinking are both uniformly attributed to individuals; of literally hundreds of references to mental acts, only four refer a mental act to children as a group (namely, as a class in school). This concreteness and specificity very strongly contribute to the reader's awareness of the plurality of styles indicated.

The diversity in styles of thinking is further illustrated by occasional overlaps. For example, Lisa characteristically reaches conclusions by means of hunches and sudden insights while Harry's inferences are generally thought out, yet both make snap judgments which turn out to be faulty. They differ again in that Lisa promptly expresses hers, while Harry's remains implicit until he is eventually led to revise it in the face of new evidence. Another example: Harry shares with Anne an ability to have insight into others, yet for Harry this depends largely upon verbal clues while Anne's are visual. Thus, while Lisa and Harry do differ, they are similar in some respects, and so too for Harry and Anne. The lack of any overt contrast between Lisa and Anne shows that the matrix of kinds of thinking is not fully articulated, thus leaving room for the reader to add in his or her own ideas on similarities and differences between the characters and their thinking styles.

The main connection between the matrix of styles of thinking and the rules of formal logic lies in the dramatic settings of the conversations of which the books are composed. There are many instances; a few examples from *Harry* will serve as illustrations.

In chapter sixteen, two main patterns of inference in formal logic, together with two related patterns of fallacious erroneous thinking, are identified by the children. These patterns are *modus ponens* which has the following pattern (where P and Q are symbols for sentences):

Suppose	If P then Q	is *true*.
And that	P	is *true*.
Therefore	Q	*must be true*.

And *modus tollens* (P and Q are symbols for sentences):

Suppose	If P then Q	is *true*.
And that	Q	is *false*.

Therefore	P	must be false.

The fallacies are *affirming the consequent* (P and Q are sentence symbols):

Suppose	If P then Q	is *true*.
And that	Q	is *true*.

Thinking that therefore P must be true.

And *denying the antecedent* (P and Q are sentence symbols):

Suppose	If P then Q	is *true*.
And that	P	is *false*.

Thinking that therefore Q must be false.

As the children are working out these patterns, it is announced that one student (Jane Starr) has accused another (Sandy Mendoza) of stealing a briefcase containing a wallet. Through Jane's subsequent responses to questions, together with his own testimony, Harry establishes that although the briefcase was recovered well outside the room, Jane still had it there at 2 P.M., and that Sandy Mendoza had not left the room between 2 and 2:45, when Jane first noticed it to be missing. Harry then argues, using modus tollens: "Now, if Sandy has taken the briefcase then it would still be here in the room. But is wasn't found in the room. Therefore, Sandy didn't take the briefcase." Lisa then remarks that she believes another student, Mickey Minkowski, took the briefcase. This idea is described as a hunch, and she tries to justify it by claiming that hiding the briefcase where it was found is "just the sort of thing Mickey would do." Tony Melillo next shows this argument to be a case of fallaciously affirming the consequent: "If it was Mickey who took the briefcase, then he would have hidden it behind the water fountain. Second part true: *no briefcase was hidden behind the water fountain.* But what follows? Nothing. We already agreed that just because the second part is true, you can't prove that the first part is also true." Now Sandy drags Mickey onto the scene, insisting that Mickey admit to having taken and hidden the briefcase.

Here we see both illustrations of rules of formal logic and a juxtaposition of discursive thinking with intuitive thought. When the children discussing the rules first learn that Jane has accused Sandy, they are told that Sandy denied taking the briefcase, that although he admitted to having teased her earlier about taking it, he had not actually done so. Jane's accusation is thus similar to Lisa's accusation of Mickey, and we have the following outline of contrasts: Jane's hunch (incorrect) versus Harry's use of the modus tollens rule (relevant to who did it), Lisa's hunch (correct) versus Tony's pointing out a fallacy of affirming the consequent (not relevant to who did it). The episode closes with a hint of the good reasons approach. Lisa admits that her idea was just a feeling, a kind of hunch, and a teacher replies: "Yes, Lisa, you made a shrewd guess. And as it happened, you were right. But if you'd been wrong, another innocent person, like Sandy, would have suffered. You weren't actually wrong to have tried guessing who might have done it. But guessing isn't a substitute for careful investigation. What it all amounts to is that I don't like reckless accusations." An *accusation*, of course, may well be supported by reasons other than deductive ones; Jane had some reason to suspect Sandy, and Lisa's hunch had indirect inductive support.

Another example occurs in chapters two and three of *Harry*. Tony Melillo shows himself to be unhappy, and in response to Harry's inquiry remarks that his father always talks as if he (Tony) will become an engineer as is the father, and that when Tony suggests that he might do something else when he grows up, his father gets angry. Harry asks Tony why his father believes that he will make a good engineer, and Tony replies: "Because I always get good grades in math. He says to me, 'all engineers are good in math, and you're good in math, so figure it out for yourself.'" Harry realizes that concluding from this that Tony is to be an engineer violates a previously discovered rule of conversion: "Your father said, 'all engineers are good in math,' right? But that's one of those sentences which can't be turned around. So it doesn't follow that all people who are good in math are engineers." Later, in chapter three, Tony has a conversation with his father. Tony asserts that from the sentence "all engineers are good in math" alone, it does not follow that he should be an engineer, even though he is good in math. Challenged to explain this, Tony momentarily forgets Harry's account, is confused and afraid, but then recalls the rule. When his father questions the rule, Tony admits that he cannot explain why it works. His father then draws a diagram of concentric circles for the sentence "all engineers are people who are good in math." As a result, Tony concludes that "that's the reason we can't turn sentences with 'all' around ... Because you can put a small group of people or things into a larger group, but you can't put a larger group into a smaller group."

This use and justification of a rule of formal logic at first seems rather straightforward, but a closer examination shows a wider less simple context than first appears. In one sense, Tony's thinking obviously improves. He learns to spot a fallacy and, in the process, successfully overcomes some fears and confusions. But from a broader perspective, this improvement has its limitations. Tony is happy with his father's explanation of the rule of conversion, and does not question this new rule of interpretation. His advance in his thinking is thus confined to replacing a confusing and uncomfortably disordered situation with a pleasing rule-governed one — he shows no sensitivity to potential limits of rule-governed thought. For example, insofar as his confusions and discomforts stem from his fathers pressures on him to become an engineer, he has not yet met this source of difficulties; if anything, he has resolved one point of confusion in a style no doubt quite similar to his father's own, and in that sense is now all the more like him than before. Tony's discomforts when confronted with suggestions that he should grow up to be like his father thus remain untouched by this rule of formal logic and its interpretation, and the two contrasting modes of thought remain at odds — semiarticulate though highly developed feelings versus rule-governed discursive thoughts.

There are many more examples. In *Harry* alone, twenty-two rules are cited, eighteen of which are standard rules of formal logic. And a related set of analyses using the good reasons model would reveal a truly immense number of comparisons and contrasts between verbal thinking which is structured by principles of formal logic, verbal thinking which can be judged by one or another set of procedural standards of the good reasons model, and the many sorts of mental acts and related styles of thinking, both verbal and nonverbal, which compose neither formal deductions nor nonformal arguments.*

4. FORMAL LOGIC AS AN AID TO PHILOSOPHICAL THINKING

Through taking part in thoughtful, reflective discussions, children gain confidence in their ability to think on their own. As a consequence, they more carefully assess things others say to them as well as their own remarks. These are self-reinforcing processes; once the children get going they can become strikingly good at constructive philosophical thinking. But what can assist them in getting started and provide sufficient initial successes to encourage them to go on to think for themselves? Here, formal logic can lend a hand.

---

*An earlier version of the foregoing material appeared in *Teaching Philosophy,* Winter, 1976. Reprinted with permission.

a. *How can Formal Logic Help?*

If you have ever taken a logic course, it is very likely that you are amazed and skeptical about the claim that formal logic can be used to encourage children to think for themselves. Because logic is so often taught as a bare set of rules to be memorized and then applied in trivial or nonsensical exercises, it might seem to develop the very opposite of reflective thinking. Here we see the primary importance of *how* the subject is presented and taught in philosophy for children.

Throughout much of *Harry* and *Lisa*, it is the *children* who discover and test the structural rules of formal logic, and who discover applications which show how the rules can be used. Further, these rules are not presented as arbitrary statements in an abstract system, but instead are discovered individually in a broad variety of settings. Not until late in *Harry* do the children begin to see that the rules can fit together systematically, and it is half-way through *Lisa* before they discover something about how they do so. Finally, and most important, the rules are not presented as formal logic at all, but rather as rules for how to think, to think well, to really think. Since so many other styles of thinking are also exhibited in *Harry* and *Lisa*, the rules appear in a very rich blend of contexts through which the readers can come to perceive limitations of the rules as well as their applications.

Here there is much that the teacher can contribute, both by pointing to the dramatic contexts in which the rules are discovered and applied, and by encouraging the children to contrast the styles of thought and mental acts which use the rules with those which do not. Since each character represents a different style of thinking, one way to do this is to ask the children what the various characters in the novels think of the rules — which ones approve of the rules and tend to use them, which do not, and why. Or the teacher can encourage the pupils to come up with situations in which a given rule applies and then to try to find others in which it does not or in which it is violated. Finally, and most important, the teacher can encourage the pupils to come up with situations in which a given rule applies and then to try to find those others in which it does not or in which it is violated, or alternatively, the teacher can look for such situations herself. It is far easier to stimulate critical thinking about something if one is oneself aware of some of its limitations as well as proper uses; it is easier to develop critical thinking in others if one is thinking critically oneself.

It is in just this simple yet profound change in perspective, from textbook examples and exercises to discussing and imitating discoveries in a philosophical novel, that encourages real children in the classroom to think for themselves while they're there. Thus, while it may not make much sense to expect a given group of live children to come up with rules of formal logic strictly on their own, it is vitally

117

important that they think of those rules as something *discoverable* by children — however imaginary — and especially that they find their own examples to illustrate and test the rules. In designing these examples, the live children are guided by the models of the imaginary children who often struggle but eventually succeed in illustrating a rule, testing it on a new case, or finding a limitation to its range of application. This encourages real children to think each rule to themselves; perhaps for the first time in their lives they begin to listen carefully to their own thinking. But here a word of caution is necessary.

Because their examples are products of their own thinking, children are particularly vulnerable to criticism if one should misfire. On one hand then, a teacher must take care not to destroy by inadvertent criticism the first fruits of self-conscious, rule-governed thinking. But on the other hand this vulnerability does help sensitize the child to coming to see the inadequacy of a lame example. Before challenging a child's example, a teacher must establish a relationship of trust and mutual respect for opinions among the children in her class and between those children and herself. First discussing the illustrations and tests of the rules provided by the imaginary children in the novels yields just the sorts of topics that can enhance such trust and respect when those discussions are handled with care.

Formal logic can contribute to the development of critical thinking because its rules are rules about sentences. Acquiring and using such rules can readily encourage children to think about what they and others say, and to use the rules as norms for evaluating claims and counterclaims. Its virtues are that its rules are clear and precise, and represent clearheaded thinking. When properly used, these rules give conclusive results or else show why no such outcome can be attained with the information given. Use of the rules can thus help foster critical thinking, but such thinking is not yet *philosophical*. Critical thinking only becomes philosophic thinking when it is aware that there are limitations to its own critical standards. In the case of formal logic, this requires a recognition that a good reasons approach to a given situation can be the more appropriate, and an awareness that non-logical types of thinking also have integrity and worth. Thus, the earlier suggestions that the teacher challenge the children to think about situations in which rules of formal logic do not apply ought not be viewed as a useful device for teaching formal logic, but should instead be understood as a basic technique for encouraging the development of truly philosophical thinking.

b. *Why Syllogistic?*

In order that a formal logical system be helpful in developing philosophical thinking, it should contain rules that are easy to use.

118

They should have a clear scope of application, but also be such that children can recognize exceptions without too much effort. Since children of ages ten to fourteen have developed some sense of differences between subjects and predicates, one system that suggests itself for this age group is *syllogistic logic,* a logic which separates sentences into subject and predicate noun phrases preceded by "all," "some," or "no," and joined by a form of the verb "to be." So, for example, the sentence "all green dragons are fire breathers" fits this bill: the subject and predicate noun phrases are "green dragons" and "fire breathers," they are preceded by "all," and joined by "are." Another example is "some race horses are fast starters," and "no cats are mice" yet another. Sentences which contradict syllogistic sentences are also covered by the rules of the system — thus "some green dragons are not fire breathers," "no race horses are fast starters," "some cats are mice" are governed by its rules.

Sentences which do not directly conform, such as "first impressions are deceptive," can often be rewritten or reconstructed so as to fit (as with "all first impressions are deceptive experiences"). Rewriting sentences so that they fit the rules of a logical system is called *standardization.* Standardization leads right to the difference between critical and philosophical thinking, since recognizing sentences to which the rules of syllogistic do not apply is a big step toward becoming aware of the limits to using such rules as critical standards.

While the boundaries to syllogistic logic have been drawn in different ways by different philosophers, there is general agreement that many sentences cannot be thus standardized. Sentences with singular subjects are conspicuous cases, as in "Jesse James was an outlaw." Other types resisting standardization include sentences expressing relations, such as "Ronald is to the right of Jimmy;" sentences with mixed quantifiers, as in "Everybody loves someone;" and especially sentences which in general do something other than describe, such as "Please don't stand on my foot," "I promise I'll be there," and "You can't go out today." Since children will doubtlessly run across such sentences (in and out of *Harry* and *Lisa*), they can eventually be helped to recognize such exceptions, and may even perceive some on their own.

Another reason for using syllogistic as a formal logic in philosophy for children is that its rules can throw light on mental procedures that have become habitual. For instance, children at an early age develop the ability to classify, but rarely do they see why classifications fit together in ways that they do. Many important sequences of classification patterns conform to the rules of syllogistic, for example, the sequence "All dogs are mammals, all beagles are dogs, therefore all beagles are mammals" fits a syllogistic rule of inference. Learning the rules of syllogistic logic can thus help children understand classifications, and encourage them to use classifications in ways that make sense.

A final but quite important reason for using syllogistics is that its rules are simple. They are tolerably easy to state and to remember, there are not too many of them, and they do not require a prior knowledge of logic or philosophy. This reason and those previously mentioned make a case for starting with syllogistic logic in philosophy for children, and so have heavily influenced the writing of both *Harry* and *Lisa*. But this is not to say that syllogistics is the only conceivable formal logic which can be used to encourage children to think philosophically. Teachers familiar with logic may want to start with some other formal approach, but before doing so should compare that system with what has been said here about syllogistics, and should have strong reason to believe that the alternative will better serve the interests and abilities of their pupils while working with *Harry* and *Lisa*.

c. *Relevant Properties of Logical Systems*

A system of rules of logic can help foster clear thinking because such systems have features akin to such thinking. Among the main properties of a formal system relevant here are *consistency* or the absence of contradictions, *truth preservation* or the ways its rules characteristically avoid going from true sentences to false ones, and *coherence* or how the rules all hang together as a systematic, unified whole.

1. CONSISTENCY

The rules of syllogistic logic do not permit a sentence and its contradictory to be asserted together. For instance, the sentence, "All cats are mammals" and its contradictory "Some cats are not mammals" are not *both* permitted under the rules. If we accept the first sentence as true then the rules require that we do not accept the second. Likewise, if we accept "Some cats are not mammals," then the rules require that we do not accept "All cats are mammals." The rules do not tell us which sentences are true and which are false, but they do tell us that *if* we accept a sentence *then* we cannot also accept its contradictory.*

---

*— In syllogistic logic, contradictions take the following two forms: "All A are B" versus "Some A are not B," and "No A are B" versus "Some A are B." To see how the rules prevent contradictions, consider the following illustration: Among the rules of syllogistic is the rule of conversion mentioned earlier in this chapter, which says that if a true sentence begins with the word "all," then its reverse is false. Thus, if we take "All penguins are birds" to be true, "All birds are penguins" must be false. One can see that this rule assumes that the subject

In some important ways, the consistency of formal logic is like the sorts of consistency we expect of one another in everyday life. If a person were to assert something but then deny it without explanation, others would very likely be struck by the fact that the person had contradicted himself. And, as we saw in the discussion of consistency in Chapter IV, they would then have good reason to suspect that he had not really thought about what he was saying. It is just such verbal inconsistencies which the rules of formal logic are designed to exclude, and that study of those rules can help bring to light.

As mentioned above, there are sentences which elude standardization under syllogistic rules, and inconsistencies involving actions, as described in Chapter IV, are beyond the scope of formal logic. The kind of verbal consistency which syllogistic promotes is thus quite restricted in direct application. Nevertheless, when children think philosophically about the rules of syllogistic, it heightens their sensitivity to verbal inconsistencies and can help them become more aware of other inconsistencies as well. Thinking about rules that exclude them, contradictions are all the more glaring when they do appear; learning to think philosophically about those rules encourages children to seek reasons when faced with an inconsistency, rather than simply be baffled or frustrated by it.

2. TRUTH PRESERVATION

The rules of syllogistic, as do all rules of formal logic, forbid transitions from true sentences to false ones. To be precise, *it is not possible using the rules to make transitions from true sentences to false ones.* As a consequence, they do not permit any transition which concludes by representing a false sentence as though it were true. The rule of conversion cited above, that if a true sentence begins with the word "all" then its reverse is false, illustrates truth-preservation: it says that no transition from a true "all" sentence to its reversal is permitted which represents the result as though *it* were true.

---

and predicate noun phrases must differ in the sentences to which it applies — this makes sense in the case of "All penguins are birds," for some birds, such as wrens, jays, and cardinals, are not penguins. If syllogistic *didn't* have this rule of conversion, then the reversal of any true "all" sentence could be true. Given that "All wrens are birds" is true, we would now be led to think that "All birds are wrens" could *also* be true, even though these subject and predicate terms differ. Since the terms differ, supposing that "All birds are wrens" is true then permits us to say that "Some wrens are not birds" must also be true. But "Some wrens are not birds" *contradicts* the original sentence, "All wrens are birds." Can the same contradiction arise in the same way if the rule of conversion is included as a syllogistic rule? Clearly not, for that rule forbids moving from the true sentence "All wrens are birds" to saying "All birds are wrens" is also true; instead, it says that "All birds are wrens" is *false*. Thus, absence of this rule brings about a contradiction which presence of the rule prevents; preventing contradictions results in preserving consistency.

Here are two examples from Chapter Five of *Harry:*

"Look," he said, taking from his pocket the bag of candies, which was still almost full. "Suppose you didn't know what kind of candy was in this bag. And then you saw me take out three pieces of candy, and they were all brown. Would it follow that there were other pieces still in the bag that weren't brown?"

"You mean would I know what color the others were without seeing them? No, I guess I wouldn't."

"That's *right!*" Harry exclaimed. "If all you know is that *some* of the candies in the bag are brown, you can't say what color they *all* are, and you certainly can't say, because some *are* brown, that some must not be!"

Here Harry draws out two syllogistic rules. First, that no transition is permitted from a true "some" sentence to an "all" sentence with the same subject and predicate noun phrases which presents the "all" sentence as though it were true, and second that no such transition is permitted from a true "some" sentence to a "some ... are not" sentence.

Truth-preservation is closely related to consistency. A rule which fails to preserve truth is a rule which allows inconsistencies. In spite of this similarity to consistency, the property of truth-preservation makes its own special contribution to philosophy for children.

Thinking about rules which preserve truth, children can become more sharply aware of passages of thought which misrepresent false sentences as true ones. An example from *Harry:*

"Lisa got on the bus in the morning to go to school, and to her delight found Fran on the same bus. The two girls chatted together for a few minutes. Then they became aware that the two men sitting in the seat in front of them were talking rather loudly, and seemed angry about something. The girls were about to decide that the men were just talking about politics, when they overheard one of the men say, "This country is really going to the dogs. And it's all because of these people who're always agitating for their civil rights. Every time I look in the paper, I read about some lawyer defending some radical. Did you ever notice how all the lawyers in this country are in favor of civil rights? And did you ever notice how all the radicals in this country are in favor of civil rights? So what more proof do you need that all lawyers are radicals?"

Fran quickly opened her notebook and wrote in it:
All lawyers are people who favor civil rights.
All radicals are people who favor civil rights.
Therefore, all lawyers are radicals.

And underneath, Fran wrote the example which she had used the other day:
All minnows are fish.
All sharks are fish
Therefore, all minnows are sharks.

She showed her notebook to Lisa and Lisa squealed with delight: "I know, I know — I noticed the same thing. It didn't follow then that all minnows are sharks, and it doesn't follow here that all lawyers are radicals."

The scene, of course, involves fictional children. And one might well want to quarrel with the broad generalizations presumed in the argument. But the moral should be clear. When children use syllogistic rules in the style of philosophy for children they can become far more sensitive to errant passages of thought. Learning to think philosophically about truth-preserving rules encourages children to look for reasons when confronted with fallacies or verbal deceptions, instead of remaining unwilling victims of careless or misleading claims.

3. COHERENCE

The rules of syllogistic fit together as a *coherent system*, sharing a common subject matter through the special types of sentences which conform to them. Three different accounts of coherence are presented in *Harry* and *Lisa*. First, the rules are described as expressing mathematical relationships between sets or classes, second as expressing the logical meaning of special words ("all," "some," "not," and "are"), and finally as illuminating certain ways of thinking. The first two interpretations of the rules have an important bearing on evaluating the syllogistic system by means of the contemporary standards of formal *symbolic* logic. These considerations bear directly on moving into more advanced logic, and could be subject matter for an eventual course on the high school or college level. But coherence in the third sense, as bearing on specific patterns of thinking, is directly relevant to philosophy in your classroom.

Harry and *Lisa* are studded with individual discoveries of logical rules. Although from a more advanced standpoint can one classify all these rules as syllogistic, neither the characters in the book nor the real children reading about them have the benefit of this higher perspective; it is an open question whether the investigation of such rules will lead anywhere. In response to this uncertainty, some of the characters demand that an explanation be given for the patterns revealed by the rules.

Two such examples stand out in *Lisa*. In Chapter Six, Harry and Tony sketch out pairwise arrangements of three distinct phrases, so as to form three different "all" sentences. To their surprise, they soon discover that not all such combinations are consistent. After they tell Fran and Lisa about their discovery, Lisa makes the following remark: "All you guys can show is that one arrangement works and the other doesn't — but you can't explain why, so what's the point?" In Chapter

Nine, Tony presses for a similar explanation: "Heather, you said you'd tell us how you figured out the correct arrangements. I want to find out what the rules are. Aren't you gonna tell us?" These *challenges to explain why certain patterns of thinking are validated by the rules while others are not, are demands for coherence.*

Seeking coherence does not of itself explain these sentence patterns and arrangements, but it does establish a criterion of *intelligibility:* that any such explanation must show how and why it makes sense to think in the patterns governed by those rules. To say that the rules must be coherent in this sense is to say that some such account can be given, that the rules are *worth* investigating on their own, and that their investigation will result in satisfying insights into the thinking they govern. As the rules of syllogistic are predominantly exhibited in the children's *own* patterns of thinking, coherence in the sense described here supports the conviction that the children's own patterns of thought are intelligible and worthy of careful attention.

d. *Ages and Stages — Why Syllogistic Between 10 and 14?*

Formal logic can help develop philosophical thinking when properly taught, but there are few real life situations to which its rules apply unambiguously. It is not just that a system of formal logic applies only to certain types of sentences, but more importantly that one rarely has *need* of its rules. The contributions of formal logic to developing philosophical thinking lies less in applications of its rules, and far more in encouraging special traits such as a sensitivity to inconsistency, a concern for truth, and a sense of respect for the thoughts of others. And these traits do apply in situations far beyond the scope of formal logic.

Given that formal logic can help develop these traits in children of ages ten to fourteen, it is tempting to ask: Why these ages? The answer though is simply that syllogistic has worked with children of these ages. It would be a mistake to suppose that this proves that syllogistic is the only formal logic appropriate to such children. Philosophy for children is presented in novels which contain a rich variety of philosophic themes, only one of which is formal logic. Thus, the success of using syllogistics at this age level may be better explained by reference to non-formal features of the books which happen to appeal very strongly to such children. Further, in watching videotapes and visiting classes, we have often been struck by the complexity of reasonings displayed by the children as they use passages of thought far more sophisticated than syllogistic rules. It doesn't follow from this, of course, that children can successfully master the more complex rules to which these passages conform, but these observations do suggest that the rules of syllogistic are not of themselves adequate to their patterns of thinking.

There have been a number of psychological studies of children's logic, most notably by Piaget. While this research has been highly suggestive for our work, it has given us no reason to presume that syllogistic is the only type of formal logic children of ten to fourteen can do. It is one thing to show that children can use this logic with profit, and quite another to insist that they can work with no other.

5. NONFORMAL LOGIC

Formal logic, presented as material for philosophical thinking, encourages children to develop a sensitivity to consistency, a concern for truth, and respect for the thoughts of others. These are all characteristics of reasonable, reflective persons. But formal logic is not the only way to encourage children to think for themselves. Together with formal logic, *Harry* and *Lisa* contain a second kind of logic, the good reasons approach. This logic uses normative rules, principles which govern two types of procedures: looking for reasons, and evaluating reasons found. This kind of logic is termed nonformal rather than informal, to emphasize the fact that while good reasons thinking often does not conform to the rules of formal logic, it does not violate them either, as does fallacious thinking. The principles of nonformal logic carve out their own area of reasonable thinking, one rarely overlapping with that of formal logic.

a. *The principles of nonformal logic*
In contrast to formal logic with its systems of rules governing the structure of sentences, good reasons logic has no such systems of abstract rules. Instead, it uses normative principles which put general constraints on the sorts of reasons that can be put forth in support of an action or opinion. In describing these principles as normative, we mean to point out that they state what *ought* to be done in the process of inquiry, or how a reason *ought* to be evaluated when inquiry is completed. These principles divide into two main classes, those which bear on the process of inquiry by which reasons are arrived at, and those which have to do with evaluating resultant reasons.

An inquiry can concern anything at all: a source of curiosity, bother, delight, perplexity, interest, irritation, intrigue. Where and how inquiry arises is a fascinating subject, but one which lies beyond the scope of this logic. Nonformal logic begins when there is something to inquire about. Seeking reasons involves becoming aware of perceptual, verbal, and evidential implications of the context in which the inquiry takes place, and drawing them out as inferences. It is here that one can begin to talk about different *types* of nonformal inferences: inductive, analogical, explanatory, action-guiding, authoritative, etc. More will be said about these different kinds of nonformal reasons below; for the present it is useful to stay with the general features of nonformal logic.

Much as already been said in Chapter Six, Part IV, about procedures for discovering implications, and it need not be repeated here. Nonformal logic places the following restrictions on these processes of inquiry. This is the first of the two groups of principles of nonformal logic.

Impartiality: The process of inquiry ought to be impartial, avoiding looking at the situation in question with bias or prejudice, or in ways which ignore the comments or suggestions of others. Seeking for reasons should be done in a fair manner, so that all concerned have a voice in results.

Objectivity: The process of inquiry should be objective, avoiding preconceived versions of the results to be gained, and staying with the relevant implications wherever they may lead. An inquiry is objective if it meets with the approval of the relevant community of inquirers, but not if it violates their sense of what counts as reasonable.

Relevance: The reasons obtained in the process of inquiry must be relevant to the issue in question, they should relate to the purpose of the inquiry. Every inquiry has some aim or goal, and this ought strongly to influence what is counted as significant and what not in the search for reasons.

Respect for Persons: The process of inquiry should be conducted in a style which avoids injuring or embarrassing anyone. Since each person is a source of significant reasons, any process of inquiry which deeply disturbs someone so as to place them outside the scope of the ongoing inquiry eliminates a potential source of information and inevitably distorts the process itself.

Search for Further Reasons: The process of inquiry should be conducted in such a way as to invite other members of the community of inquirers to search for further reasons, if they find that they are not satisfied with its results. This requires that whatever process be used, it be sufficiently open-ended so as to invite further inquiries rather than discourage them or shut them off.

Each of the preceding restrictions presupposes that the inquirers share an intuitive sense of what is to count as reasonable. It would be a mistake to try to formulate this too precisely; it need not be pictured as some mysterious inner intuition, but simply as a rough sense of what is reasonable and what isn't. Just because it is ill-defined, people may disagree on what is or is not a violation of one of these restrictions, but such disagreements are usually confined to borderline cases.

An example of a shared inquiry in which such a borderline case appears is in Chapter Seven of *Harry*. While searching for reasons why Dale should or should not have to salute the flag, Suki proposes that he should, because "rules are rules." Mrs. Halsey, who is moderating the discussion, accepts this as implying that if we make rules we should keep them. Mickey then responds: "No,' he insisted, "rules are made to be broken. Don't you know the expression, 'every rule has an exception'? Well, Dale's case is the exception! Therefore I think Dale doesn't have to salute if he doesn't want to." Mrs. Halsey criticizes this use of "every rule has an exception," implying that it is too idiomatic to be relevant to the purpose of the inquiry. But, as Tony, Sandy and Mark then show, a case can be made for its relevance: rules of conduct not made by the people to whom they apply can have exceptions in situations where those people don't *want* to obey them. This leads to an impasse, and the reader is left to speculate on whether or not "every rule has an exception" can be interpreted as supplying a reason why Dale shouldn't have to salute the flag.

The discussion is a good example of a nonformal inquiry, and there are several others in both novels. Each chapter, at least in part, has some such inquiry embedded in it, some encouraged by adults, but most directed by the children themselves. Together with the discussion with Mrs. Halsey mentioned above, two of the best examples of nonformal inquiry are in the last chapter of *Harry,* with Mr. Spence, and the last chapter of *Lisa,* with Mr. Partridge. Though the children often engage in nonformal inquiry on their own, this is usually spaced out in separate sequences rather than concentrated in a single uninterrupted search. An example of a compact sequence is the row of discussions about doing to others as they do you, in Chapter Fourteen of *Lisa.*

In practice, the process of nonformal inquiry and the evaluations of reasons discovered are often combined, with inquirers moving back and forth from one set of procedures to the other. But it is useful here to separate the principles of nonformal logic into the two groups of searching for reasons and evaluating them, since these principles have different areas of application. There is a natural tendency to equate reasons with *good* reasons, to suppose that a reason for believing or doing something can't really *be* a reason unless it's a good one. But this ignores the fact that we sometimes do things for bad reasons (rather than no reason at all), and that we can compare reasons as better or worse. And this points to the second main group of principles of nonformal logic.

Nonformal logic provides the following standards for evaluating reasons:*.

Generality: A good reason is a reason expressed in general terms. To see that a reason is a good one, one should be able to see what it would mean to use that reason in situations other than the context in

---

*For a related analysis, see John Rawls, *A Theory of Justice* (Harvard University Press, Cambridge: 1971), pp. 131-135.

question. This requires that a reason cited must apply to a variety of situations, hence that the reason itself be stated in terms sufficiently general to give it breadth of application.

Universality: A good reason is a reason for every member of the community of inquirers. They may not all agree that it is a good one, but each can see for him or herself whether it applies to the action or opinion in question, and when they agree that it does this standard applies.

Publicity: A good reason is a reason known to every member of the community of inquirers. As in the case of universality, this does not mean that everyone has to think it's a good reason, or even that it is worth considering. But they can know of it and so have a chance to react to it, and when this is the case the standard applies.

Order of Conflicting Claims: If there is a conflict within the community of inquirers as to which reasons are good and which are bad, a good reason will be a reason which imposes an order on the competing claims, showing how in the given situation certain of the views expressed are better reasons, and others worse. This may not completely resolve the conflict, because even after the good reason has been accepted a disagreement may remain among members who proposed the more reasonable views. But a reason which refines a disagreement — and perhaps resolves it — is a good one.

Finality: No reason is a good one which does not meet one or more of the above standards, and every reason must be evaluated, or at least be open to evaluation, by the members of the community of inquirers. There is no higher court of appeal, nor higher standards in evaluating reasons.

Taken separately, each of these standards invites criticism. With sufficient ingenuity, one can no doubt construct a situation in which a standard will be *violated* for good reason. To develop philosophical thinking about the standards, it is well worth one's while to try to imagine such a situation for each of them. This is indeed important, but it is also important that one not miss seeing their collective significance. Taken together, these standards and the group of restrictions on the process of inquiry outline how to transform a class of pupils into a community of inquirers who participate in shared dialogues. There are certainly many more dimensions to developing such discussions, particularly in nonverbal and affective domains. But striving to use these rules in class discussions, especially by encouraging your students to think for themselves by means of these principles, will go a long way to encouraging your students to think independently while sharing their thoughts, to become reflective reasonable people capable of exercising good judgment.

As in the case of the restrictions on the process of inquiry, these standards also presume that the inquirers share a rough sense of what is to count as a good reason. Use of the standards is then much less a matter of presenting something new and wholly unfamiliar, and far more one of encouraging children to sort out, from among their many responses to an inquiry and its results, those which are the more useful and appropriate. This in turn raises questions about the teaching of nonformal logic.

b. *Teaching nonformal logic*

Children are wonderfully inquisitive. So long as their native curiosity has not been completely discouraged from showing up in class, when philosophy is introduced they soon develop the ability to seek reasons on their own. The main effort in teaching nonformal logic consists of bringing to bear suitable restrictions on the process of inquiry, and of eliciting standards of what are to count as good reasons.

How should the procedures of nonformal logic be taught? It is surely a mistake to suppose that the children can learn the principles of nonformal logic by memorizing them as a set of abstract formulas. First, both the process of inquiry and the evaluation of reasons are *activities,* and so can properly be mastered only by performing them rather than by stating principles which regulate them by heart. Second, the principles can only be understood through taking part in shared inquiry. A further look at them shows why.

In contrast to the rules of formal logic which clearly apply to the internal structure of certain sentences and arguments, *no nonformal principle completely describes its scope of application.* Consider, for example, objectivity in the process of inquiry: "An inquiry is objective if it meets with the approval of the relevant community of inquirers, but not if it violates their sense of what counts as reasonable." All well and good, so far as it goes. But how far *does* it go? The rule doesn't give the slightest hint as to what members in a given community will count as reasonable, and what not. The restriction only begins to make sense once one actually engages in shared inquiry. Take, as another example, the standard of universality for evaluating reasons: "A good reason is a reason for every member of the community of inquirers. They may not all agree that it is a good one, but each can see for himself or herself whether it applies to the action or opinion in question, and when they agree that it does this standard applies." Members of the relevant community must decide whether the reason applies, but the standard gives no clue as to how they are to do this. As with the principle of objectivity, the standard of universality can only begin to make sense when one is a member of such a community, engaged in shared inquiry.

A close look at each of the principles will show that they can only be understood in the context of a community of inquirers who take part in

129

shared dialogues. It is not just that the principles only make sense given such a community; they are a part of its structure and outlook. So, it is only through having such discussions that children can begin to discover the procedures the principles represent, and come to judge their worth.

In sum, teachers can discuss these principles with their pupils any time at all. There is certainly no need to view them as some sort of "hidden agenda." But they ought not expect the children fully to understand the principles or see the point to using them until the children themselves have taken part in shared dialogues. In this sense, good reasons principles cannot be directly taught at all, but must instead be elicited from the children as they become adept at shared inquiry.

Teaching nonformal logic requires using the procedures its principles represent while encouraging dialogues. This in turn depends on having material available that can invite such discussions, and this is just what the philosophical themes in the novels are designed to provide. By reflecting on the opinions and actions of the characters in the books, children are encouraged to draw their own inferences, to compare and contrast them with those of others, and so to begin in shared inquiry. To help them do this effectively, two models of inquiry can be presented to the students: the illustrations of good conversations in the novels, and exemplary discussions in their classroom.

While a good deal has already been said in Chapter Six about running good discussions on philosophy, some important features of encouraging dialogues are particularly relevant to teaching nonformal logic, and deserve reemphasis.

Children are not in a position to evaluate a reason for something unless they know what that something is. So they need to learn to listen to themselves and to each other as they talk about the topic in question. Similarly, they've got to get a hold of the reasons offered, and have time to think about them in the context of inquiry. Both of these requirements make very strong demands on the teaching of nonformal logic. Encouraging children to listen to themselves means taking time to listen and to remember — there is no more effective way to encourage children to listen to themselves than by listening to them and remembering what they have said.

Getting children to listen to one another takes more time, and it especially takes patience. So often they tend to revert to looking to the teacher for an evaluation of what another child is saying, and to ignore it if it does not meet with an instantaneous sign of approval. In overcoming this habit, they can come to replace it with the impression that anything goes, that whatever comes to mind can and should be said, with no regard for the theme of the discussion or the other members of the class. It can take a great deal of patience to weather these reactions. Again, the best and strongest resource is the teacher's own memory; it can always be in the power of a teacher to recall what went on before a digression set in, to ask how a comment bears on prior remarks and opinions, and so to encourage students to stay with the subject — not least by sticking to it oneself.

Learning to listen to oneself and to others in the community of inquirers is essential to mastering the procedures of nonformal logic, and so of learning its principles. Impartiality, objectivity, respect for persons and searching for further reasons all depend upon paying careful attention to one's own thoughts as well as those of others, to developing the discipline of a well-trained ear. Generality, universality, publicity, ordering conflicting claims, use of these standards requires a well-developed ability to pay attention to others as well as to oneself. More can be said about the relevance of other discussion techniques for successfully teaching nonformal logic, but the main connections between teaching nonformal logic and the use of such techniques should now be apparent.

c. *Types of nonformal inferences*

Earlier in the chapter, it was mentioned that nonformal logic involves becoming aware of perceptual, verbal and evidential implications. In the context of an inquiry, these are drawn out as inferences. A nonformal inference thus states a reason which stands in a certain relationship to the action or opinion at the focus of inquiry. There are many such relationships within the scope of nonformal logic, such as inductive, analogical, explanatory, action-guiding and authoritative inferences. This list is by no means complete, but it does represent the major types of nonformal inferences. To examine each in detail would require a book-length study in nonformal logic, but a survey of some main features of these types of inferences can help fill in the picture of what nonformal logic is about.

Inductive inferences typically proceed from specific to general statements, where the generality projects beyond the evidence base cited in the specific cases. Some examples appear in Chapter Five of *Harry*. First, certain inductions are criticized. "Maria looked thoughtful. 'But people are always jumping to conclusions. If people meet one Polish person, or one Italian person, or one Jewish person, or one black person, right away they jump to the conclusion that this is the way *all* Polish people are, or all black people, or all Italians or Jews.' 'That's right,' said Harry. 'The only exercise some people get is jumping at conclusions'." Mark Jahorski then proceeds to make an induction with somewhat more respectable support. He cites his own experiences in his school, and reports from kids in private and parochial schools, in support of his generalization, "the schools are awful everywhere." As is typical with nonformal inferences, he could well be wrong, but the diversity of reports that agree with his opinion give him something approaching the standards of publicity and universality, and in that sense this evidence approximates a good reason for his generalization.

An analogical inference presupposes that there are relevant similarities between two different types of things, and concludes to a further similarity. A cluster of analogical inferences occurs in Chapter One of *Lisa,* concerning similarities between people and animals. For instance, hunting is compared and contrasted with killing people — some children accept the presumption that people and animals are sufficiently similar to warrant the comparison, others reject it: "Randy shook his head vigorously. 'You just have to remember that people and animals are completely different. It doesn't matter what you do to animals, but you shouldn't do the same things to people'." This leads to a discussion of whether animals have rights. They never reach unanimity, and though the children do recognize each others' reasons as reasons, there is no clear indication whether they think any of them are good ones.

Explanatory inferences are answers to the questions "Why did that happen?", or "Why does this take place?" They presume that nature exhibits a certain regularity or is made up of certain things, and that the event to be explained is an instance of that regularity or is produced by those things. Take, for example: "Why did the light go off?", an explanatory answer to which might be, "I flipped the switch." For people who know about connections between switches and lights, this is a reason, and in an appropriate context it can be a good one. Explanatory inferences are contrasted with descriptions in Chapter Fifteen of *Harry,* but no specific examples of explanations are cited. Many explanatory inferences make use of scientific knowledge, and investigating differences between good explanations and bad ones leads directly to the philosophy of science.

Action-guiding inferences justify what someone has done or is doing. These inferences can presuppose either a system of practices, a rule of conduct, or that there are special circumstances which justify violating a rule of conduct or a system of practices. A recurring theme in *Lisa* is Lisa's own search for reasons as to whether she ought to eat meat or not, and this involves evaluating several action-guiding inferences. For example, she is aware that her family has customarily eaten meat and enjoyed it; this is a system of practices which can justify meat-eating, but she is not sure it is a good reason. As Lisa accepts the analogy between animals and people mentioned above, she is deeply troubled when she realizes that animals must be killed in order to sustain the system of practices. This inclines her to refrain from eating meat due to the special circumstances on which the action is dependent — she views it as something close to a good reason for violating the system of practices, but is still troubled by the question of what she ought do. Finally, she hits upon the following rule of conduct: "If I really love animals, I won't eat them" (Chapter Fifteen), which, to her eyes at least, justifies her action of avoiding meats by stating a good reason for not doing so. Problems of evaluating action-guiding inferences can lead to ethics and moral education; this is discussed in the chapter following this one in this book.

Authoritative inferences, inferences from authority, warrant their conclusions by referring to some authority as the source of their claims. Such an inference presumes that the authority cited is a reliable source of information concerning its conclusion. Authoritative inferences differ markedly from the other types of nonformal inferences discussed above; there are special problems in assessing inferences from authority, and applying good reasons standards to their claims.

In cases of inductive, analogical, explanatory and action-guiding inferences, it is not very difficult to imagine how to use them to foster philosophical thinking. Take, for instance, an inductive inference, such as Mark's, that concludes: "the schools are awful everywhere." One can ask live children to assess that inference by asking them to assess the adequacy of its evidence base, for example, by asking whether any of the other children in the novel enjoy going to school (there are several hints in *Harry* that suggest some do). Similarly, with any inductive inference whatsoever, one can ask one's pupils to compare its evidence base to its generalization by encouraging them to describe circumstances under which it is an appropriate generaliza- tion, and then to describe circumstances under which it is not. Since inductive inferences characteristically project beyond available evidence, the children can eventually discover that there is no simple mechanical answer to the problem of distinguishing good inductions from bad ones. They can then be encouraged to try using the good reasons standards as a means for evaluating inductive inferences. Something quite similar to this can be done with analogical inferences, explanatory inferences, and action-guiding inferences. In each case, one can move from encouraging children to examine certain inferences critically to encouraging them to think philosophically about evaluating such inferences and distinguishing good ones from bad. But it is not at all obvious how authoritative inferences can be treated in this way. Since authoritative inferences depend on the reliability of their sources, asking children to evaluate an inference from authority seems to put them squarely in the position of having to judge the reliability of the authority to which it appeals. This is a particularly serious issue, since children would rarely seem to be in a position competently to examine the credentials of any adult authority. To see just how the good reasons approach can be used to evaluate authoritative inferences, we should first consider the broader context in which this problem of evaluation arises.

d. *Some problems of authority*

Children are repeatedly confronted with demands on what they should think and how they should act, demands often accompanied by the assumption that children need to be told these things because they cannot judge them on their own. Sources of these pronouncements have traditionally been parents, ministers, other relatives, and teachers, but these authorities are now in many instances competing with others such as peer groups and public figures who equally share in the assumption that the children they influence must depend on them for guidance. And children are becoming increasingly exposed to the subtle, ill-defined, hidden authorities of television. Given this confusing barrage of authoritative claims and directions, what are children to do?

One proposed solution is that each child should be encouraged to ignore all authorities and instead rely strictly on his or her own experiences. Telling children to trust in experience rather than other persons may seem to have a toughmindedly scientific ring, but it is certainly *not* scientific; scientists continually depend on observations and experiments made by other scientists, and typically do their work in special communities in which they share research interests with other scientists, trusting in these others to evaluate the significance of their own research results. In any case, however toughminded it may be, telling children to trust solely in their own experiences puts an intolerable burden on their shoulders. It projects them into separate solitary existences, and works to cut them off from developing a sense of cooperation and of mutual respect, an awareness of what others can contribute to their lives, and a concern for the well-being of other persons.

But if children are not to ignore all voices of authority, how are they to distinguish the better, more helpful authorities from the worse? This problem remains insoluble so long as children are put in the position of having to judge the worth of other people. Instead, they need to learn to separate what is said from the person who says it, to learn to judge the worth of *what these persons say rather than who they claim to be.* Here, the good reasons approach can help.

As children learn that they are able to search for and recognize good reasons, they are encouraged to pay more attention to what an assertion says and less to the person who makes it. This gap widens as reasons are discovered which support the assertion, especially as they come to perceive whether the reasons discovered are good ones or bad. Thus, as children begin to sense the internal authority of their ability to think for themselves, they develop standards for recognizing *reasonable* authorities. These are people willing to offer reasons for what they say, and, when questioned, to try to show that their reasons are good ones in the style of nonformal logic.

Consider now how this bears on the problem of evaluating authoritative inferences. For example, in Chapter Ten of *Harry,* Jill Portos gives the following reason why Dale should not have to salute the flag: "I think Dale ought to stick by his beliefs, because — because that's what my father says, and he ought to know." Mrs. Halsey questions whether Jill's father is a special authority on the matter in question, such as a lawyer or a judge. "No, but he's awful smart," replies Jill.

Mrs. Halsey then responds: "I'm afraid that that won't do. You should only use someone else's opinion as a reason for your own view if that other person is a recognized authority on the subject in question." This gives one clue to the evaluation of an authoritative inference: in citing an authority it cites a *reason* for its conclusion. But how are children to evaluate such citations? According to Jill, her father *"ought* to know," but according to Mrs. Halsey, he is not a *"recognized* authority on the matter in question." These are sharply differing evaluations of the reason Jill cites. Can children ever resolve such disagreements?

The second clue to the evaluation of inferences from authority lies in the contributions other types of nonformal inferences can make to such evaluations. Whatever the authorities cited say, if they themselves are reasonable people then *they have reasons* for what they tell the children and *these reasons can be assessed through the good reasons approach.* There is a hint of this in Jill's response to Mrs. Halsey: "No, but he's awful smart." There is a suggestion here that her father has reasons for saying what he does about Dale, but there is no clue as to whether Jill is aware of them or not, or whether they are good ones.

There are three ways to go about evaluating an authoritative inference. First, one can ask the authority cited for reasons in support of the conclusion, second, one can ask a like authority for such reasons, and third, one can try to construct reasons on one's own. In each of these cases, once reasons in support of the claim made by the authority are forthcoming, they can be evaluated as giving inductive support, or as using some analogy, as explanatory, action-guiding, etc. Of course, all three of these evaluative procedures run the risk of deception, either by the authority questioned or through the third technique which can result in a mere rationalization. But this risk diminishes as children develop the ability to think for themselves, for example by combining these procedures and testing the results for consistency.

6. HOW MUCH TIME SHOULD BE SPENT ON LOGIC?

First one must have a clear understanding of the difference between promoting good discussions and teaching nonformal logic. Teaching nonformal logic involves paying special attention to types of nonformal inferences such as those discussed above, critically examining them and evaluating them. That the principles for evaluating such inferences bear on what is a good discussion is no coincidence, but there is a vast difference between using those principles to promote such discussions whatever the topic, and using them to evaluate nonformal inferences.

With this clarification in mind, how much time should be spent on logic in a program of philosophy for children? The question cuts two ways — how much time should be spent on logic instead of other topics in philosophy, and how much time ought one spend on logic for it to be properly taught? It is very important to keep in mind that logic is a means for presenting *philosophy,* rather than the other way around. It is one of several philosophical topics, and should not be thought of as the fundamental subject at the expense of all others.

Logic is a means for presenting philosophy to children because it can be used as a vehicle for encouraging philosophical thinking. As we have seen, this applies to formal as well as nonformal logic. But logic can do this only insofar as the teacher is comfortable with the subject. There is no more important criterion regarding its use. Teachers who believe that their students should learn logic, but who do not themselves feel at home with the subject, should resolve that problem before trying to teach logic. Teacher training in philosophy for children goes far in eliminating discomforts with logic; this is one of its most important functions. In teaching philosophy to children one should always keep in mind that one cannot reasonably hope to encourage reflective thinking, much less recognize it when it takes place, unless one feels at ease with the topic under discussion.

Other things to consider in response to the question, "How much time on logic?" are the students' own needs and interests. As to formal logic, one should not underestimate the delight children can exhibit while playing around with the rules and finding illustrations. What to us may seem obvious or mechanical is by no means always so to children. They can play with words and sentences as they play with balls and toys, and a rule of logic, for some children at least, can be as much fun as a frisbee. As to nonformal logic, it is wise to avoid thinking that the children will not learn it at all unless it is made a separate topic of instruction. Embedded as it is in the procedures of dialogues, simply encouraging a class to become a community of inquirers can be a very effective way of getting across some of its main ideas.

Formal and nonformal logics differ in ways that can bear directly on the needs of your students. The rules of formal logic have the virtues of clarity and rigor, and the vice of irrelevance. At best they apply to a minor segment of everyday discourse, and even on these occasions there is seldom any real need for them. The principles of nonformal logic have the virtues of breadth of application and practical importance, and the vice of ambiguity. The principles do apply to a wide variety of situations, but not always in clear and precise ways; they can be very helpful, but can also work at cross-purposes with one another. Taking these features into consideration, we cannot prescribe the proper mix of formal and nonformal logic for your classroom. For this, teacher training in philosophy for children is indispensable.

Chapter Eight

CAN MORAL EDUCATION

BE DIVORCED FROM

PHILOSOPHICAL EDUCATION?

1. SETTING THE STAGE FOR MORAL GROWTH

Few teachers today are unaware of the expectation of parents and society that education, in addition to developing basic skills, also expand the moral dimension of the child's personality. But to do this, a teacher must become a substitute parent, and of course it is no easier for a teacher to be a surrogate parent than it is for a parent to be a surrogate teacher. In brief, the question of how a teacher is to encourage students to be moral is one of the most perplexing issues in modern education.

Educational theorists have presented the teacher with so broad a spectrum of alternative theories of the moral nature of the child that the extreme views virtually cancel each other out. On the one hand, the child is viewed as a little savage who must be tamed and domesticated; on the other hand, children are seen as little angels with impulses already moral and virtuous, so that all that is necessary is to provide the right environment for them to be themselves. A more reasonable view is that native to the child are innumerable dispositions which, if encouraged, could lead to *any* kind of human behavior, and often do. What is important is that the environment in which the child grows up should be such as to screen out those forms of conduct that do not contribute to growth, while encouraging those which do. This is not the same as the romantic view which holds that all one has to do is to provide the right environment and let children be their "naturally good" selves. In other words, a teacher has a responsibility for screening out those forms of behavior in pupils which are obviously self-destructive, and for screening in those forms which are self-constructive. The teacher may have to decide on the basis of knowledge of individual children just which features of conduct need to be encouraged or discouraged in each individual case. One child may need to be drawn out; another may need to develop more self-control. But the object is to liberate the child's creative powers of thinking and acting and making by developing his or her capabilities in ways that reinforce and strengthen each other rather than block each other or cancel each other out.

Each child is an individual and at the same time each child is part of the class. The teacher must forget neither of these facts. But they are not separate facts. As an individual the child is distinctive, and can develop his or her unique powers in terms of the roles to be played in the group. The individual distinctiveness will reveal itself in the difference that he or she makes in the classroom, and *every child in the classroom should make a difference.* Thus, in a sense, the teacher's role is to ensure that each child feels that he or she has the capacity to make a difference and each day acts on that presupposition. Ask yourself regarding each child in your classroom: "Would the absence of this child make a distinguishable difference in the classroom?" If the answer is "no," then something is definitely wrong with the way that you have conceived your teaching role in relation to that child. To the extent that you have not encouraged that child to be an active seeker of his or her own uniqueness, an active harmonizer of his or her own powers, an active creator of his or her own contributions to the class group, you as a teacher have fallen short of success.

It may seem harsh to place so much responsibility on the teacher's shoulders, but children cannot be expected to develop a sense of responsibility unless the adults that they are surrounded by, and whom they seek to emulate as models, likewise accept responsibility for what happens in the classroom. In this regard, it is worthwhile to distinguish those things that are responsible merely in the sense of being *causes* from what is responsible in the sense of being *accountable.* Thus, the child's organic impulses and native dispositions play a causal role in his conduct but they cannot be held accountable for his behavior. The child is, of course, accountable for controlling those impulses.

On the other hand, the school environment over which society has control, an environment which encourages or discourages those dispositions, is something for which society can very much be held accountable. To this extent, the moral development of children can be estimated only in relationship to the accountability of the society in which the children find themselves. A society which does not value a school environment which is conducive to moral growth (and often this is expressed just in terms of the amount of money that it is willing to invest in education) is a society that should openly accept its share of blame for the amoral conduct of its children.

Instead of relying on a child's home environment, a setting which might or might not be conducive to moral behavior, the teacher must focus on the kind of environment that can be created in the classroom. The teacher's responsibility, as has been said, is for screening in those kinds of dispositions which lead to children's growth, and for fostering interaction between the individual child and the classroom environment as a whole. (That environment includes the teacher as well as the other children.) It is a truism that a child in the classroom who has been treated in the past with condescension and contempt is now likely to treat himself or herself with disrespect. Those who treated this child in this fashion are of course accountable for having done so. But the teacher in whose classroom this child is found is accountable for seeing to it that the child find an environment which accords respect and support, so as to counteract the treatment of which he or she was a victim in the past. Another child may display a lack of imagination or curiosity, again as a result of a deadening environment or regimen either at home or in school. The responsibility of the teacher is to see to it that an environment is created for this child which is challenging on a daily basis so as to overcome the numbness and apathy resulting from his former environment. Still another child, perhaps as a result of the home environment where he or she is often the object of aggression, may resort to very aggressive behaviors towards others. It is the teacher's responsibility to make sure that this child is placed in such a setting that there is no need for him or her to engage in aggressive behavior in order to protect or to restore damaged integrity.

It is proverbial that, "the child who disturbs others is a disturbed child." But this is inadequate because it diagnoses *the child* as pathological, rather than *the situation* which produces the behavior. Thus, once the teacher begins to assume responsibility for actively creating environments which are supportive, and which lend themselves to the building of self-respect and self-mastery, a most essential step has been taken toward engaging in moral education.

Unless an environment is created which is conducive to mutual trust and respect for each individual in the classroom, no educational program, neither philosophy for children nor any other, is going to make much of a difference in helping children to become moral individuals.

2. SOCIALIZATION AND AUTONOMY IN MORAL EDUCATION

Very often, it is taken for granted that children are complex, difficult, unruly and amoral. One then infers that the child is responsible for the problematic character of moral education, rather than acknowledge that the problem of moral education is complicated by ones own presuppositions about it. But it should be evident that if we better understood just how much autonomy we are willing to accord the child and just how much control we are willing to retain and relinquish — if we better understood and were more honest with ourselves about what kind of persons we want our children to be, and what rights they have in exercising choice as to the kinds of persons they want to be — the moral development of children would be considerably less perplexing.

It is not uncommon to pose the problem of children's moral development in this fashion: either moral education must be construed as a way of getting children to conform to the values and practices of the society in which they find themselves, or education is a way of liberating children from those very values and practices so that they can become free and autonomous individuals. Such a formulation of the problem is most unfortunate, because it commits education to the kind of ideological controversy from which education itself should rescue human beings. So to pose the problem of moral growth is to gloss over the many non-constructive dispositions and proclivities of any individual, and to gloss over the many supportive and beneficial aspects of human society. Putting these value labels on society and on the individual is counterproductive, if our objective is to encourage children to judge for themselves. To think of human individuals as innately good or bad or of society as innately good or bad is to foreclose all possibility of determining through inquiry what is responsible for each situation as it stands, and how it can be improved. To the extent that any dogmatic statement about society or the nature of the individual cuts off inquiry, man is reduced to a passive unresponsible spectator rather than an active, involved and responsible shaper of the society in which he lives.

Moral education worthy of the name necessarily involves acquainting children with what society expects of them. Moreover, it involves enabling children to develop the tools they need in order to assess such expectations critically. As with the parent-child relationship, the society-child relationship is fraught with mutual duties and reciprocal rights. It is not education to present these in a one-sided fashion. Some of us tend to think of institutions as themselves repressive and that in a better world we would not suffer from institutions at all. But this is a serious misreading of the situation. It is not a question of whether or not to have institutions, but rather whether the institutions we have are to be organized in a rational and participatory fashion. When they are not, it is correct to say that the individual is at their mercy. When they are, they cease to be coercive and become constructive instruments for the achievement of individual concerns and objectives.

Acquainting children with the conduct that society expects of them is only part, although a very important part of a responsible moral education. It is also necessary that children be equipped to think for themselves, so that they can creatively renew the society in which they live when the situation demands it, as well as for the sake of their own creative growth.

When we say that education of necessity must enable children to develop the tools they need in order to assess society's expectations of them in a critical fashion, we do not mean to imply that the teacher's role is nothing more than the fostering of critical judgments on the part of students. The objective is not to form a classroom of critics, but rather to develop human beings who have the capacity to appraise the world and themselves objectively, as well as the capacity to express themselves fluently and creatively. The forming of a critical attitude is only part of the teacher's role. Students must come to realize that although being able to stand back and look objectively at the institutions around them is essential, it is not enough. If one is disposed to be critical, one must also try to propose something new and better. This is why dialogue in the classroom is helpful: it brings out the positive and constructive ideas that children are capable of generating as well as their negative ones. A teacher must be able to applaud creative insight when encountering it just as a teacher has to be able to applaud instances of logical reasoning.

Criticism can often be the springboard for the teacher to initiate philosophical discussion. For example, in *Harry Stottlemeier's Discovery,* when Mark begins criticizing all schools as bad, he launches a discussion regarding the aims of education in terms of which his classmates are then able to judge whether the schools are or are not capable of achieving those aims. The discussion culminates in their devising alternative ways of running schools so that the aims of education might be better met.

A child in the classroom might begin not with a criticism but with an imaginative alternative proposal for how things could be, but which unfortunately lacks any indication of how it is to be put into practice.

Rather than concentrate on the ineffectiveness of such an idea, the teacher should encourage the other children in the classroom to suggest specific ways in which the idea might be put into practice.

But what of ideas — creative as they might be — that the teacher judges to be destructive? E. g., suppose a child should suggest "Let's get rid of minority X as a first step to a better society." As always, the best source of the answer to such ideas should be the other children in the classroom. If the idea is genuinely unconstructive, then the critical abilities of the other children should spot the deficiencies of the idea and point them out. But suppose they don't? Should the teacher intervene? Well, the teacher always has the right to intervene and state his or her own opinion if the circumstances warrant it. What is obnoxious is the teacher introducing his or her own opinion before the children have had a chance to respond to the original proposal, thus foreclosing genuine consideration of alternatives. On the other hand, if the teacher feels that the children have been able to develop their own ideas and can hold them in a strong and confident fashion, then that teacher should not feel hesitant about introducing his or her own ideas, where the children themselves have failed to bring forth such a point of view. The children should understand that the teacher has temporarily abandoned the role of moderator in order to assume that of co-participant.

Now let's push the matter a step further. What if, after presenting a point of view, the teacher gets this response: "Well, that's only one point of view and we don't buy it!" It is here that philosophy is unique. Since it is inherently a process of dialogue, it is not under any obligation to come to a particular conclusion at a particular time. The teacher's response could be, "Well, let's talk about it some more tomorrow." Or, "I'll take your views into serious consideration and we can talk about it again."

The substance of what we have been saying is that it is unconstructive for the teacher to put himself or herself in the role of bringing about the child's submission to social values, or to assume the role of encouraging the child's individuality to give way to mindless nonconformity in the area of moral education or any other area. The teacher is a *mediator* between society and the child, not an arbitrator. It is not the teacher's role to adjust the child to society but to educate children in such a fashion that they can eventually shape the society in a way that is more responsive to individual concerns. It is important that educators recognize the plasticity of society as well as that of individuals and the necessity for community self-renewal, if society is to continue in a participatory fashion. Nothing so guarantees the inflexibility of society with respect to individual creativity as the teaching of children that society is inflexible with respect to individual creativity.

3. DANGEROUS DICHOTOMIES IN MORAL EDUCATION

Teachers today are bewildered by the overwhelming array of alternatives in moral education. There are purely cognitive approaches which portray morality as efficient reasoning. Others construe morality as obedience and acceptance of discipline, thereby making it a matter, not of intellectual reasoning, but of character. Still others interpret the child as being naturally virtuous, so that good behavior will naturally ensue if only the emotions are unthwarted and unrepressed and sensitivity to others heightened. What bewilders a teacher is that, based on experience in the classroom, it is evident that each of these positions has a degree of validity. There is an element of reasoning in moral education, as there is an element of character-building, and as there is an element of emotional liberation and sensitivity training. The problem is not to devise a program which would do any of these things but to do all of them.

If morality were simply a matter of knowing rules and obeying them, then moral education would consist in developing in children a conscientousness which would permit them to carry out these rules in a happy, unquestioning fashion. But morality is not so simple. It is not clear that there are rules for every situation, nor is it clear that it contributes to children's development that they should accept uncritically those rules which might apply. Consequently, the child must be equipped to cope with situations lacking clear guidelines, situations which nevertheless require that one make choices, and, that one accept responsibility for the choices which one makes.

We have been stressing that, in the area of moral education, the teacher must do much more than acquaint the child with the predominant values and morals of that society. The teacher must involve children in a process that will insure that they learn to think for themselves, that they be trained to read the cues and signs of other people's interests in situations in which they are involved, and that they become aware of their own emotional needs. We do children a disservice if we hold them responsible for behaving in a particular way in a particular situation when we have given them no practice whatsoever which would develop their capacity to deal appropriately with such a situation when it comes up. This is one reason why programs in moral education that emphasize moral *thinking* are insufficient. They fail to develop the patterns of constructive *conduct* which make moral behavior something children can readily engage in when the need arises for them to do so. Unless such patterns are developed beforehand, each new moral confrontation becomes traumatic for children, because they have not been given preparation in moral practice. Moral education is not just helping children to *know* what to do; they have to be shown how to *do,* and be given practice in *doing* the things that they may choose to do in a moral situation. Without such doing, moral education breaks down. Nowhere so much as in moral education is the bond between theory and practice, knowing and doing so, so important — yet nowhere is it so often disregarded.

Children find themselves in various situations during the course of a day. Some of these situations call for action, some do not. But children can hardly know what actions or decisions are called for or appropriate unless they have developed an awareness of the dimensions of each situation, its complexity and its various nuances and subleties. If children can become aware of the requirements a situation places upon them and the opportunities it offers them, they can respond to it appropriately and effectively. We therefore emphasize the importance of calling children's attention to what is involved in the various life situations they face, as a prerequisite to their intelligent response. Once they grasp the meaning of a situation, they will better know what they want to do.

But we can hardly expect children to carry out their response effectively if they have not been able to prepare themselves through various forms of moral practice. We can hardly expect children to be tactful in moral situations where tact is called for, if they are unfamiliar with tactful performance. There are situations that call for a young person to encourage another child, to console another child, to express gratitude, to advise, to reconcile. Yet children can be mute and inarticulate and passive with such demands upon them, because they have had no practice in performing in these ways, or even in imagining how they might perform. Exercises in moral practice are therefore important supplements to sensitization of the child to the moral aspects of situations.

But it is not enough to criticize the dichotomy between thinking and doing and to recognize the need for both in an effective program of moral education. It is equally necessary to insist upon the indissoluble bond between thinking and feeling. There is little value in instructing a child in what would be universally right to do in a given situation when the child doesn't care about anyone, let alone everyone. It is hard to see how a child who is not interested in other people's feelings would have any sympathy with their needs, or how one who is not in the habit of putting oneself in other people's places would be the least bit interested in acting in accordance with moral rules even if they were known and accepted. Moreover, the feelings necessary to moral conduct are not restricted to particular sympathies for this person or that person, since it is equally indispensable that one be sensitive to the entire situation of which one is a part. Such sensitivity may require the most delicate awareness and capacity of discrimination. It involves an ability to appreciate what a situation requires and what might be appropriate to those requirements. It requires the capacity for considering as fully as possible the consequences of one's behavior. Often, what we condemn as immoral behavior may simply be the result of a certain insensitivity to the character of the situation in which one finds oneself and one's lack of capacity for seeing oneself in relationship to the whole. The morally inconsiderate person is often one who has failed to take all things into consideration before acting. The tactlessness of a child in the classroom is often due simply to a lack of a sense of proportion, in which individual needs and feelings which should be placed in the context of the needs and feelings of everyone, are instead accorded absolute priority.

Now the teacher may ask, "How can I develop this kind of tact and sensitivity in my pupils?" Here is where the heightening of aesthetic perception can lead to a greater moral awareness and sense of proportion. For example, a child may have difficulty picking up cues about what is going on in a meeting, or he might be incapable of seeing how his talents and insights can play a contributory rather than monopolistic role in a certain group. He still continues to view his relations in an egocentric rather than social sense. Instead of endlessly moralizing about the need to develop sensitivity, empathy, a feeling for "what is going on" without giving the child any definite tools to develop these traits, involvement in the type of dance activities called kinetics, or the type of musical activity (chime activities, choral activities, group work of one kind or another) which calls for listening to the notes of others and then attempting to play an appropriate sound, often results in the child's beginning to develop the necessary sense of proportion which he might be lacking.

An assumption frequently made is that the child's intellect is educable but his feelings are not. Human emotions are assumed to be primitive and irrational. One can tame and domesticate them, but one cannot cultivate and refine them, much less use them in cognitive enterprises. They are simply brute forces, and one must use all the wiles and strategems of one's intellect in order to discipline and control them. This is a very curious view of human emotions. If our desires and feelings were not educable, we would never want better food, better friends, better art, better literature, better communities. The theory of the ineducability of human feelings and desires flies in the face of the fact that people do learn to desire more knowingly and more reasonably. Instead of always pitting intelligence over and against feelings, an educator should focus upon making desires more intelligent and intellectual experiences more emotional.

To separate the affective and cognitive in moral education is treacherous and is to misunderstand the nature of learning. Our own conception of intelligence is not a "mentalistic" one. We do not see intelligence as something that takes place in the "mind." Rather, intelligence can be displayed in any form of human behavior, in one's acts, in one's artistic creations and in one's reflections or verbalizations as well.

Today, when a teacher hears the word "affective," all sorts of things are suggested. In the realm of affective education, expressing one's feelings, getting things off one's chest, baring one's soul, letting off steam, all seem to be part of the picture. Such an approach implies a patronizing view of human emotions. The image is of a person building up too much emotional pressure and then finding release in some harmless escape. In this way, the emotions are dispersed and the force that they might have provided for the child's constructive activities is lost.

On the other hand, an alternative and equally mischievous view regarding affective education is that the affective is superior to the cognitive and should be the primary focus of all education, including moral or value education. Such a view has no more to recommend it than its polar opposite just discussed. The school that fails to sharpen children's cognitive skills condemns such children to be helpless to deal with those aspects of life situations which call for rational analysis. The result is a fatuous dwelling upon affective behavior, with no development of the skills essential to making a difference in one's society or to making an imprint on one's world. If we fail to develop their cognitive skills it is paradoxical of us to hold children morally responsible for their behavior.

Another dichotomy which is an underlying assumption of many moral education programs is the dichotomy between fact and value. This assumption has often led teachers to believe that somehow value education can be treated as a self-sufficient and autonomous discipline, separated from the different subject areas of the curriculum, and that it is valid to separate "facts" from "values" as though they were two different things, facts being "objective" and values being "subjective."

Thus, we have a time during the days when we explore and clarify our values (a personal, subjective enterprise) and other times when we explore and clarify facts (an objective social enterprise.) But the teacher who is compelled to deal with values by themselves in this detached fashion often finds that it is an area of curiously bloodless abstractions, or even worse, an endless discussion of children's demands for "what we want," and "what we desire," rather than of "what matters are really of importance to us."

While we urge that children be given practice in reading aright the individual character and significance of the individual situations in which they happen to find themselves, in no way do we assert that moral values are merely subjective, or merely relative in the sense that any response is as right as any other for a given situation. We deplore the fashionable doctrine that in matters of value, "Everything is relative; what may be right for you may be wrong for me, and that's the end of it!" To assert this is equivalent to saying that anything goes.

Our stress upon logic and inquiry is meant to counter this subjectivism by giving children some of the tools which they can use to analyze the situations in which they find themselves, so as to come to sound and reliable conclusions. Children who have the opportunity to discuss their feelings with one another can proceed to analyze those feelings and understand them more objectively. As they develop habits of thinking carefully and critically, they reach out more systematically for factual evidence, and begin to consider alternative ways of acting, rather than merely basing their judgments upon hearsay, first impressions or "subjective feelings."

To assume that facts and values are separate is treacherous in its implications for moral education. Given this separation, it is easy to suppose that one can change one's values without a change in the facts of one's situation. But this is an illusion. It is futile for a teacher consciously engaged in moral education to hunt for certain disembodied entities called "values," or to encourage children to eke out such entities on their own when, in fact, all that is meant by the term "value" is *a matter which is or should be of importance to the child.* All too often, children encouraged to clarify their values end up talking about their feelings and wants, rather than assessing the *objective worth* of what their feelings and wants are about. For example, children might say that they feel much more positive about being in the playground than about being in school. What a philosophical discussion should bring out is what the objective differences are between playgrounds and schools, so that children can assess the importance of each, and under what circumstances one is to be preferred to the other. Values should not be identified as a person's desires but as those things which after reflection and inquiry are found to be matters of importance. Thus the process of inquiry moves from a subjective to an objective orientation.

In the perspective of perceptual observation, this round bit of copper is identifiable as a "fact": in the perspective of economic matters, this same thing is the least valuable of our coins — and is therefore an economic "value." That you are now reading this page is a fact. That you find it worthwhile to do so makes reading the page not just a fact but a matter of value. The existence of the apples you consider purchasing is a fact, but the store identifies them as "fancy," and thereby cites their grade of "value." So fact and value are nothing but the same thing viewed in different *perspectives.*

For purposes of analysis, we can isolate an order of "facts," and likewise, for purposes of analysis, we can isolate an order of "value," but matters that concern us are always at the intersection of those orders. There are not two different things, "facts," and "values": there are simply matters which are simultaneously factual and valuational. This is essential for a teacher to understand, because it is the teacher's responsibility to see to it that children do not disconnect moral ideals from moral behavior. This separation often occurs when children are encouraged to talk about values as if they were independent and self-sufficient entities divorced from the world of fact, instead of talking about courageous behavior, fair behavior, respectful behavior, right behavior and just behavior in particular situations.

On the other hand, we should not assume that children are incapable of talking *about* morality. That children can analyze moral issues does not exclude their discussing abstract ethical concepts such as "fairness," or "rightness," since children are able to function on a theoretical as well as on a practical level.

4. WHAT TO DO TO HELP THE CHILD KNOW WHAT TO DO

The teacher's role is not that of a supplier of values or morals, but that of a facilitator and clarifier of the valuing process. The child who comes to realize the uniqueness of many moral situations will be able to discover that no moral rule can be uniformly helpful in determining what to do, Insofar as previous educational experiences have challenged this child to improvise and invent where rules have been lacking, such ingenuity will stand him or her in good stead. However, the appropriateness of children's actions is to a great degree dependent on their understanding of and personal commitment to the valuing process itself. Thus, the fact that a child might have to come up with a new solution in a particular moral situation in no way excuses that child from being concerned about his or her motives, society's expectations or the probable consequences of the action.

The teacher, in the role of facilitator and clarifier of the valuing process, must introduce children to certain criteria by which to judge whether or not an action is moral. Such criteria can enable children to reflect on

a) how this action affects them;

b) how it affects the structure of their habits and character;

c) how it affects the direction of their lives;

d) how it affects the other people around them and

e) how it affects the institutions of the society of which they are a part.

149

These measures or criteria become the guideposts which the teacher can use to steer the children towards some kind of cumulative understanding of the nature of particular actions.

However, it is always important to keep in mind that moral situations are not necessarily routines to which routine solutions apply and that moral criteria must be reevaluated constantly and reconstructed to make them relevant to the times. It is this openness with regard to criteria and moral actions themselves that sets the philosophically oriented" teacher apart. The realization that often situations are opportunities for innovation (and such innovation could well involve a going beyond the call of duty rather than merely living up to it) must always be kept in mind. Thus, it follows that the teacher should concentrate on helping children engage in moral reasoning for themselves and not merely pass along to those children the values of society or the teacher's own values.

We do not mean to say that every personal, moral situation is unique. Situations can have much in common, and when they do, rules that have generally worked in like cases can be expected to work again. What we *are* saying is that the child should be equipped to distinguish like from unlike situations, usual from unique situations, typical from atypical situations. The child should be prepared to confront the different or unprecedented courageously, resourcefully and imaginatively, rather than try to impose upon the unusual situation a rule that is doomed to fail.

So long as the child cannot distinguish similar situations (to which rules based on past experience may apply) from dissimilar situations (which require that unique solutions be devised), the whole question of the role of rules in moral behavior is moot. The sensitive discrimination of similarities and dissimilarities among situations is of fundamental importance to the child's moral development. The child must be able to take into account a large number of subtle and complex features of situations — their metaphysical, aesthetic and epistemological as well as their moral aspects — which are present whenever we compare or contrast such situations with one another. We cannot expect to encourage children to respect persons unless we acquaint them with the full implications of the concept of a person, and this requires philosophy. Nor can children be expected to develop an ecological love of nature without some philosophical understanding of what "nature" is. The same is true of such terms as "society," "thing," "wealth," "truth," and countless other terms and phrases which we constantly employ, but of which the child generally has only the most diffuse understanding. Comprehensiveness is what philosophy in its broad sense tries to provide. More than anything else it is comprehensiveness which moral education — in the traditional sense of rule-inculcation or in the conventional sense of "decision-making" or "value-clarification" cannot provide.

5. IMAGINATION AND MORAL EDUCATION

To many people moral reasoning is confined to logical reasoning, that is, to drawing conclusions from premises or from factual evidence. But moral reasoning should not be so narrowly defined. The role of imagination in moral reasoning is of utmost importance.

Of course, this would hardly be so if the solution to moral problems could be worked out in a purely mechanical fashion as one might pose an arithmetical question to a computer and have it display an answer. Very often, wrongdoing is not the result of someone's malice, but merely of that person's inability to imagine a constructive or creative approach to a predicament. For example, two decades ago the spread of polio had reached serious proportions and there was considerable panic among parents. When it was announced that a polio vaccine had been invented there was widespread relief. But the Department of Health, Education and Welfare promptly provoked a blast of criticism by confessing that it had ordered only a relatively small number of doses. The Secretary of HEW responded: "Who would have thought that the public demand for polio vaccine would be so extensive?" For an official in a position of responsibility to make such a remark would seem to represent a failure of moral imagination, to say the least.

Moral problems are a sub-class of human problems in general. It takes imagination to envisage the various ways in which an existing unsatisfactory situation might be transformed. One has to be able to visualize what would happen if this were to be done or if that were to be done, or if nothing were to be done at all. In other words, imagination is needed to anticipate the goals and objectives which a moral individual or a moral community might seek.

At the same time, it takes imagination to review the alternative ways in which each of these goals might be achieved. What steps would have to be taken? What materials would have to be employed? Who would have to be involved? What must be done first, and then secondly, and so on? And what would happen as a result of the employment of each of these alternatives? It takes a vivid imagination to rehearse all of these possibilities. But in so far as morality is the planning of conduct, then it exhibits very much the same characteristics as any kind of successful planning does. One can't plan without imagination. One can't plan a business venture without imagination and one can't plan one's conduct, if it is to be successful, without imagination. Now it is evident that the kind of conduct we prefer children to engage in is the kind we should encourage them to practice. Likewise, it seems plausible to expect that exercises in moral imagination could very well develop a readiness in the child for dealing imaginatively and creatively with situations which otherwise the child might find perplexing and bewildering.

Exercises in moral imagination consist of two major varieities; first, there are those which involve consideration of different types of means-end relations, and secondly, there are those that involve different types of part-whole relations. Getting children to practice breaking down a problematic situation into its parts, then imagining how it could be transformed into an improved alternative, is a combination of both of these varietes. Children have to be encouraged to exercise imagination with regard to each of the facets of solving moral problems.

a. *Imagining means-end connections*

Such practice in moral imagination of the means-end variety can be formulated in a cooperative fashion: for example one might engage the class in an exercise such as this:

1. Imagine someplace you would like to visit. Write it down and exchange papers with your neighbor. Now let your neighbor write down all the things he or she can think of which you would have to do in order to get to the place you want to go, while you write down all the things your neighbor would have to do in order to get to the place he or she wants to go.

Suppose, for example, your neighbor says she would like to visit her grandparents in a city that is 3000 miles away, and would like to stay there for a week.

You might write something beginning like this:

First of all, you want to arrange transportation. You may want to go by airplane. So you have to get tickets. Find out how much they will be. Do you have money to buy them? If not, maybe you will have to use a cheaper means of transportation.

Next, you will have to decide what you will need to wear at your grandparents'. You will have to have some kind of luggage to take it in, too. You will have to prepare your clothes, etc., etc.

2. Perform the same exercise, only imagining the following:
   a. What you would like to be someday.
   b. What you would like to do tomorrow.
   c. The kind of "best friend" you'd like to have.
   d. What kind of community would you like to live in?

3. Are there things you have now which you wouldn't want to change at all? Name some of them.
   a..
   b..
   c..

152

In the first part of this illustration, children are encouraged to think of where they might wish to go as an imaginary exercise. They are then made to see by their neighbors that such wishes are ends which require means for their implementation, and the neighbors spell out these needs. How well the neighbor does in this task will again depend upon a capacity to visualize and anticipate the practical aspects of getting something done. Thus, this is an exercise in encouraging children to specify an imaginary end and then requiring them to cooperate in the imaginative construction of the means of achieving such ends.

b. *Part-whole connections*

Similarly, moral imagination requires encouraging children to consider how wholes can be broken down into parts, and how parts can be used to build imaginary wholes. Of course, if the teacher doesn't know how to do this, it will be impossible to transmit the art to a child. For example, suppose you are considering admonishing a child who has been disruptive by sending him to the principal or counselor. A segmental view of this situation would involve your merely directing this admonition to the child. But you can hardly neglect consideration of the larger context of your actions, namely, how will this action be viewed by the class as a whole and how consistent will it be with the remainder of your behavior towards that class? Thus, your action is not just between you and the disruptive child but involves the totality of interrelationships in the classroom.

An example of the part-whole exercise in moral imagination might be the following:

Suppose, (as editor of the school newspaper), someone has suggested to you that you run a contest to see who is the prettiest girl in school. You decide to talk this over with the editors of the newspaper, and one of the editors points out that this would probably get people to read the newspaper, and that's good. But another editor asks what the effect of this will be on the school community as a whole. Your class can take it from there. The questions that it can raise include: what is meant by pretty? why is the contest limited to girls? how do the losers feel when the contest is over? Is it worth having a contest when so many people might feel badly? Is the kind of competition which is encouraged by this sort of thing healthy? In other words, one tries to see a particular activity as a part of a larger frame of reference.

We talked earlier about the necessity for the creation of an environment of trust, mutual respect and cooperation in the classroom as a precondition of any meaningful moral education. But what kind of activities can you as a teacher come up with that will involve all of the children in your class, each in a different or unique way, in a cooperative enterprise which, in turn, can begin to create this kind of

153

mutually respectful environment? To conceive of the class as a community, the teacher has to be prepared to imagine various divisions of labor within the class that will offer individual children distinctive roles in that community. You have to see the parts within the whole, just as you have to be able to construct a whole out of the parts.

Needless to say, one of the most useful ways of stimulating a child's moral imagination is to place him in situations which call for innovative conduct, although they are not specifically moral. Discovery-type situations in science classes are of this character, but even more helpful are dramatic or dance situations in which inventiveness on the part of each participant is encouraged. A ballet, for example, where one of the dancers comes up with a novel movement can excite the entire group to respond, each in his own way, although what they do does not have to be lacking in composition or coordination. Every time a child paints there is the need to work from parts to wholes and to analyze wholes into parts. The same is true with writing a poem or any other instance of artistic creation. What the teacher concerned about moral imagination must be prepared to do is to help the children relate these instances to one another. The teacher can point out that the heroic deed discussed in a literature or history class was creative; an act that took the same kind of imagination as a remarkable innovation in one of the arts. We are not all called upon to be heroes, just as few people are great artists, but every moral problem presents a need for some degree of imagination if its reconstruction is to be effective to all concerned.

c. *The role of models in moral imagination*

One of the virtues of the philosophy for children program is that the novels the children read, such as *Harry* and *Lisa*, are in effect model communities of children. They are not so idealized that children reading them cannot identify with the characters, while at the same time, they provide models of intelligent discussion among children as well as between children and adults.

The novels also provide models of inquiry, models of cooperation and models of caring, sensitive individuals. What this does for the student is demonstrate the feasibility of such an ideal children's community, where the participants are intellectually and emotionally wholesome, lively, and actively involved. A student having no inkling of the possibility of ever interacting with such comrades in such a situation is deterred from using his own powers of reflection, cooperation, and discussion. One reason why children are often taciturn or reticent, even to the point of being withdrawn, is perhaps that they cannot see the feasibility of using their powers in a constructive fashion. They are often creatures of fear, anxiety, and pessimism.

A model community, even though fictional, converts such fears into hope. It lets the child know of the imaginative possibility of a world where people relate to each other in a way that evokes the creative possibilities of each individual. The model therefore stimulates children's moral imagination. They may never have known what they wanted or what they sought. The model helps them understand their own needs, their own desires. They begin to see that this is *how things could be*. And they can begin thinking seriously of alternative means which can be explored and examined in an effort to achieve something like the ideal which they have now glimpsed.

However, the ideal is not held up for the child to imitate in a docile or uncreative fashion. A young artist wishing to be like Rembrandt would not think that his life task would be the slavish copying of Rembrandt's paintings, but would seek to be true to his own situation the way Rembrandt was true to his. To emulate a model is not to imitate it or copy it but to use the model and allow it to stimulate those feelings of hope, courage and belief in oneself which might enable one to live as effectively in one's own unique and creative way as the children in the novel live in theirs. So models are enormously useful for the stimulating of moral imagination in the child, which in turn liberates those constructive feelings and energies that can be converted into moral activity.

6. WHERE TO BEGIN

Perhaps a word should be said about "moralizing." To help children develop morally does not require that, at every possible moment, one point out to students the moral implications of what they are doing. Children have every justification for finding such behavior on the teacher's part difficult to tolerate. From an educational point of view, it is counterproductive, for it sets up a situation in which the child recognizes a patronizing and condescending attitude towards his or her own moral capacities. The child's strategy of self-defense is to seek ways to challenge or test the teacher's interpretation of the situation and the battle is on.

In order for a moral education program to be adequate, it must enable the child to think reasonably, develop patterns of constructive action, become aware of personal feelings and the feelings of others, develop sensitivity to interpersonal contexts, and acquire a sense of proportion regarding one's own needs and aspirations *vis-a-vis* those of others. Obviously, this is a huge task for any teacher. The teacher may well throw up both hands and say, "This is more than I can do. How can I even begin to go about it?"

The teacher can begin by helping children develop habits of logical and critical thinking, by encouraging them to engage in philosophical dialogue where they can discuss their opinions and feelings with others and at the same time learn about other people values and points of view, and by giving them the opportunity to engage in individual and collaborative inquiry where they can appreciate the values of objectivity, impartiality and comprehensiveness, values that are indigenous to the philosophical enterprise. By encouraging children to engage in moral practices, by allowing them more and more responsibility in the classroom, on the playground and in the schools as a whole, coupled with exposure to all other aspects of philosophy, they gradually can begin to make sense of the moral dimensions of their world.

How much autonomy should a child be given? Neither more nor less than what he or she can handle at a given moment. It is up to the teacher constantly to assess and reassess what children are capable of handling, thereby providing an opportunity for them to test and retest their capacities. The word "responsibility" often has an unpleasant connotation for children, because they associate it with their liability to being blamed if they do not do what they are supposed to do. This is a most unfortunate interpretation, because it is only insofar as children are given more and more responsibility for dealing with the conduct of their lives that they acquire any modicum of freedom. The child who thinks of freedom as the opposite of responsibility has bought the same misconception that his parents may have accepted: that freedom is merely getting away with not doing what one is supposed to do. This interpretation, characteristic of immature individuals, equates freedom with license. The misguided child thinks of freedom as not doing what grownups want rather than seeing that freedom resides in doing what one *upon adequate reflection and inquiry* desires to do in a particular situation. However, children can seldom realize this unless they are given more and more opportunities to have some say over their own behavior, and to have some input into the decision-making processes of the group to which they belong.

Thus, "Children's Rights" from the viewpoint of the child, means the child's right to say, "I want more and more responsibility, as I am able to handle it with regard to my own conduct. To deny me the opportunity to discover what is appropriate conduct, to deny me the opportunity to be responsible for myself, is to keep me a perpetual child, dependent on others for setting up the laws and rules of my behavior. It is to deny me that experiential foundation of freedom and responsibility which is essential if I am ever to think for myself with regard to morality." Obviously *the role of the teacher is to gauge the rate and timing of the child's acquisition of this enlarging capacity for assuming responsibility.*

7. WHY MORAL EDUCATION CANNOT BE DIVORCED FROM PHILOSOPHICAL EDUCATION

Now it may be asked "What has all of this to do with philosophy for children? How will philosophy for children accomplish this moral education? How is it different from other methodologies now available to teachers?" In the first place, philosophy provides a regimen for thinking, so that the logical aspects of the moral situation can be dealt with by the child who has learned how to unravel the logical aspects of a situation and can see the need for objectivity, consistency and comprehensiveness in his or her own approach to such situations. Secondly, philosophy involves a persistent search for both theoretical and practical alternatives, with the result that the encounter with philosophy generally leads the child to a more open and more flexible attitude towards the possibilities in a given situation. Thirdly, philosophy insists upon awareness of the complexity and multi-dimensionality of human existence, and systematically tries to point out this multi-dimensionality to children so that they can begin to develop a sense of proportion about their own experience. It stresses the fact that a problem situation is seldom merely a moral situation, but has metaphysical, aesthetic, epistemological and other such aspects. Consequently, as the child comes to engage more and more frequently in the practice of considering life situations fully and exhaustively, i.e., taking into account their many dimensions instead of treating them superficially, he or she becomes more and more sensitive to the complexity of such situations and the need to take into account as many of their dimensions as possible. Fourthly, philosophy for children involves not just reasoning about moral behavior, but also the devising of opportunities to practice being moral. This contrasts with programs that stress decision-making or the making of choices by the child, in that it seeks to prepare children for moral life by developing those competencies which they need in order to do what they choose to do. The exercises in moral practice which form an integral component of the philosophy for children program give children an opportunity to act out how they would engage in forms of behavior which often have a moral dimension, such as consoling, caring, advising, honoring, sharing, etc. We cannot expect children to be considerate if we do not give them opportunities to learn what "being considerate" is through allowing them to practice engaging in such conduct. Exercises in moral practice are primarily designed to involve the child in doing. We can exhort the child to care and to be considerate, and we can even show the logic of this behavior, but it will avail us very little if the child does not know what actions are consonant with care and concern. *Moreover, it is not that such actions emerge naturally from a caring and concerned individual, but rather that the voluntary performance of such actions tends to develop care and concern in such individuals as perform these actions.*

This is a very important insight for the implications it sheds on the role of the teacher in the classroom. Rather than talking about considerateness, caring or any other moral virtue, it follows that the teacher's role is to set up situations in which children can actively partake of such experiences as will reveal to them what considerateness, caring and other moral characteristics are in the light of their own experience, and what people do who have such feelings, for morality consists not in the feelings themselves but in the conduct that is conjoined to such feelings.

Fifthly, we said that a sufficient moral education program would have to develop in the child an awareness of the feelings of others. Philosophy can never be separated from dialogue because philosophy inherently involves questioning, and questioning is an aspect of dialogue. When philosophy for children enters the classroom, the classroom becomes an open forum for all sorts of ideas. But it is not just a brainstorming session where all ideas can be thrown out uncritically. Philosophical discussion leads to acquaintance with the wide diversity of points of views to be found in any group, and with the equally broad set of differences among opinions and beliefs. Since offering opinions in a classroom discussion does not pose the demand for competence which is posed when the teacher asks for a correct answer to a question, children find the exchange of opinions and the disclosure of differences in perspective inviting and reassuring rather than threatening.

However, once this reassurance has been established, the teacher must assume responsibility for introducing the criteria of a philosophical discussion (i.e., impartiality, comprehensiveness, and consistency) and for making sure that the discussion itself builds and "makes a difference" for the children. Students will become rightfully impatient if too great a degree of irrelevance is tolerated. Similarly, if the discussion does not seem to have a cumulative development, students will become fatigued by it. Moreover, the teacher has to be aware that a discussion leader has to be extremely careful, should it be appropriate to endorse a particular opinion voiced by a student, not to close off further discussion and inquiry by such partisanship.

It is the teacher's role to encourage consistency in the presentations of the students, although such encouragement may take different forms. For example, in one case it might be necessary to point out to a student that what he or she is saying does not follow from what was said before by the same student. In another case, where the student's intent was evident but the presentation fumbling, the teacher may offer to restate the position in a more coherent fashion. In short, philosophical discussion, by making children aware of one another's beliefs and points of view, and by subjecting such beliefs and opinions to philosophical criteria, leads children to become conscious of one another as thinking and feeling individuals. Without such dialogue, children may sit side by side in classrooms for years without encountering one another as individuals who are, like themselves, striving to make sense of their own experience. One unfortunate consequence of this is that the child often comes to an erroneous conception of knowledge itself, thinking of it as a merely private matter. In contrast, philosophical dialogue leads children to realize that the acquisition of understanding is more often than not a *cooperative* achievement.

Sixthly, philosophy for children introduces the novel as the vehicle of moral education, as well as of education in metaphysics, logic, aesthetics and epistemology. The novel as a philosophy text affords an *indirect* mode of communication which, in a sense, safeguards the freedom of the child. Children are less inhibited when they feel that they, their family experiences, and their personal life experiences are not the focus of classroom attention. With the *distance* that the fictional technique permits, children are left free to interpret and eventually decide for themselves which philosophical views make the most sense to them, without the dread that they may fail to come up with the morally "right answer," or that the discussion process is part of a manipulative diagnosis, or a phase of a therapy session by an amateur therapist.

A sufficient moral education program must insist upon the development of both cognitive and affective capacities without making the one superior to the other. Instead of conflicting, thought and feeling can be induced to reinforce one another. Using the novel as a vehicle of exposing the students to philosophical ideas and concepts has the advantage of demonstrating the affective and cognitive dimensions of life interwoven at every moment. These ideas are then discussed in the classroom, in the context of the children's own responses to them. The progressive elaboration of ideas in the classroom dialogue continues to interweave the cognitive and affective strands of experience. For example, mastery of the logic component of the philosophy program has its affective as well as cognitive rewards: it increases children's self-confidence and ability to

159

make sense of their experience. In areas where ideas presented in the program are highly controversial (e.g., the aims of education), children begin to discover their own points of view as they listen to other people express their opinions. They also discover how ideas, when passionately expressed from one's own point of view, can vehemently attract or repel listeners.

Children slowly begin to discover that as they are able to distinguish sound and unsound ideas, a growing taste for sound ones and a distaste for unsound ones begin to emerge. That is to say, children's feelings come to be enlisted in the pursuit of intellectual understanding. In time, children come to develop a stronger desire for the more warranted assertions than for the less, for the more beautiful rather than the less, and for that which is better in conduct rather than worse. One can say at such a point that the individual has grown to have enlightened feelings and intelligent desires. Thus, the ideal curriculum in moral education would introduce to the child every philosophical concept illustrated or embodied in some affectively charged activity, and conversely would endeavor to impart to every such activity or mode of feeling an appropriate cognitive content.

With the introduction of strictly affective techniques into the classroom in the past decade, we have observed that children often are very reluctant to "bare their souls," as it were, in the public context of the classroom, nor should they have to. Often children feel under a great deal of pressure to talk about their emotions when they do not want to, for fear of being thought "up tight." If the child is reticent, the teacher may feel a need to press harder thereby assuming the role of therapist to which the teacher is ill-suited. In the end, the process can be counterproductive.

On the other hand, when children find themselves reading a novel about other children, they can feel more at ease in discussing the affective aspects of the novelistic character's life-experiences, because such affective aspects are integrated with the cognitive searchings of these fictional characters for ways of reasoning that will help them make sense of their world. As these reasoning rules are mastered, the children in the story begin to feel more self-confident and capable of expressing themselves, their ideas and their feelings.

Then as open dialogue ensues in the classroom, the teacher will probably find that the students will often reveal increasing confidence in themselves and trust in their classmates. This trust and sense of mastery can fuse, and the philosophical discussion can proceed confidently to move from the children in the novel to personal interpretations and applications should the children in the classroom feel a need and a desire to do so. Although it is the teacher's role to encourage children to see the connections between the theoretical concepts introduced and practical life problems, it is never justifiable to pry or to force any child to talk about personal emotions or personal life experiences in the context of a philosophy course.

In addition to providing an indirect mode of communication, the philosophical novel can also serve various other purposes. It can act as a model of philosophical dialogue for the children in the classroom. It can also act as a springboard for the discovery process. That is, it can hint at philosophical ideas which can then be elaborated on and developed into substantial philosophical concepts through classroom dialogue and activity. It can enable children to learn the difference between logical and illogical thinking in a relatively painless fashion, and attempt to indicate to children when logical thought is appropriate and when non-logical thought might be preferable. Another essential function which the philosophical novel can perform lies in its attempt to *sensitize* children to the complexity and ambiguity of moral situations and, at times, to the necessity of inventing or creating appropriate moral conduct. This is a role to which the novel is particularly suited. We might all admit that often we learn more about how to act and how to judge the appropriateness or morality of actions from reading and discussing novels than from reading and discussing books on moral philosophy. The novel is a form well suited to crystallizing the multi-dimensionality and complexity of moral situations and moral choices, as well as for revealing the consequences of those choices. It is in this fashion that the novel provides a vehicle for the development of moral sensitivity. To the extent that children become involved in the plot and critically reflect upon the actions of the characters, taking into account the complexity of the situations which they find themselves in and the consequences of their actions, to that extent they are involved in a process which can result in a heightened moral sensitivity — i.e., a heightened sense of appropriateness with regard to human actions. Further, the novel, as such, can often facilitate discussion among children as well as between children and teacher. It thus can become a vehicle for transforming the traditional dynamics of the classroom into a situation in which the children begin to realize that they have as much to learn from one another as well as from the teacher, and the teacher can discover how much can be learned from sharing the children's perspectives.

There are a number of educational approaches today which seek to promote classroom discussions (particularly in the area of moral education) and this of course includes the philosophy for children approach. The eagerness of children to engage in examination of their common problems makes it possible for such discussions to develop very easily and naturally, once an atmosphere of trust and mutual respect has been created. There might be little to distinguish a classroom engaged in a philosophy for children program from a classroom engaged in other moral education programs. The observer would see children expressing their thoughts or feelings, sometimes with deep conviction, sometimes merely in an effort to please the teacher or in an effort to conform to the thoughts expressed by their peers. But a more experienced observer might note two important differences. First, the philosophy for children approach deliberately seeks to keep the moral dimension within the larger context of the child's life, and to balance it with discussions of other philosophical subject areas — metaphysical, aesthetic, logical, epistemological, and so on. This is not to diminish the importance of the moral in children's eyes, but to strengthen their awareness of the other domains, so that such heightened awareness can then inform, enrich and humanize the insights they may develop with respect to moral issues. Secondly, the experienced observer would discern the constant employment by children, in their discussion of the philosophical text, of logical techniques which are conducive to more efficient and critical thinking. It is the teacher's role as the program develops to explain these logical techniques and then supply the children with exercises which help them not only to master the techniques but to apply them to situations which have meaning for them. As these logical techniques become understood and utilized by both teacher and children, classroom discussions tend to display objective progress rather than relativity or stasis.

The philosophical novel itself provides a vehicle of demonstrating that each child has his or her own style of thought and conduct. The children in the novels can act as models which reinforce the notion that children are not merely little blobs, but that each child, whether in the novel or in real life, is a person who is beginning to work out and put together a style of life and a basic direction to that life. This is essential in the education of every child, because once the child can perceive what is the basic direction of his or her own life, then that becomes the basic criterion against which one measures the choices one makes in particular situations. The child who lacks a sense of direction will treat every situation on an *ad hoc* basis. This is mindless empiricism at its worst. By steering children's conduct along the lines of the basic directions they are finding for their lives, their achievements build on one another, become cumulative, and are capable of helping children grow. Moral education involves helping them assemble and rally their energies and abilities, and directing them along the lines in which they themselves choose to develop. A sound moral education must provide strategies which the teacher can demonstrate to children, so as to help them discern the innumerable connections that exist between themselves and their peers, between themselves and grownups, and between themselves and the customs and institutions amidst which they must live.

Without awareness of such connections, children cannot be expected to understand the moral dimension of human experience, and to act effectively upon such understanding.

8. THE RELATIONSHIP BETWEEN LOGIC AND MORALITY

The reader of *Lisa* will readily recognize that not only is the book about reasoning and morality, but that it is very much concerned with the *interrelationship* of logic and morality. In the first chapter, we find Lisa noting that she loves roast chicken, and that she loves animals as well. But now she glimpses a problem: if she really loves animals, is it consistent for her to eat chicken? It is not a question here of her duties to other people; it is simply a question of the consistency she would like in her own life — among her own thoughts, and between her thoughts and her actions.

Later, the children in the book begin to complain about an invasion of their privacy of discussion, when they realize that they learned of this through accidentally overhearing the principal's conversation. Once again the problem of consistency confronts them. How can they demand privacy for themselves but deny it to others?

On another occasion, Lisa wonders how it is that Millie thinks it all right for men to marry women younger than themselves, but not for women to marry men younger than themselves — to Lisa, Millie's position seems inconsistent.

Still another instance — the children tell the principal that if he genuinely believes in education, then he will encourage them to think for themselves. But, they tell him, he is not encouraging them to think for themselves. So he must not really believe in education.

The case of Lisa finding a discrepancy between loving pets and loving to eat animals points up an important but often neglected consideration — that a crucial aspect of morality may be not so much one's values taken individually as the relationships that obtain *among* them. Lisa's affection for pets in no way obliges other people to like pets. Lisa's loving roast chicken in no way obliges other people to love eating chicken. But, Lisa suspects, she cannot live comfortably with herself while holding incompatible values. If she really loved animals, it seems to her she wouldn't eat them. But she eats them. So, she is forced to conclude, she must not really love them. The moral issue here is not one thing or the other, but the connection between them.

The person who has been taught that morality is concerned simply with the particular values which one holds on particular issues will likely fail to see much significance in the point here. Either lying is right or it isn't, he will say. Either stealing is right, or it isn't. But these are flagrant cases, lurid cases, about which we have intense anxiety, and it is very difficult for us to discuss them reasonably. Consequently we may find it very difficult to explain to a child just why we believe that not lying is right, or why not stealing is right. Focusing on the act alone is like looking at something through the wrong end of the telescope: suddenly it looks too large, out of all proportion, and we can no longer see it in context. When we focus just on the act of lying itself, without envisaging it in its connections with other acts and beliefs, when we consider the act as isolated and out of context, we suddenly find we are talking about an abstraction. Yet we feel so strongly about it that we cannot think of any other way to deal with it but to insist upon its wrongness more and more vehemently. Unfortunately, this gets us nowhere with the child we are trying to educate morally.

Nothing is easier than to disregard the connections among our values, but in so doing we disregard the basic structure of morality. As Harry Stottlemeier and his father note in one of their discussions, it is possible to take a large-scale social event culminating in some atrocity, and dismember it, isolating into discrete, simple and morally neutral acts all that preceded it and contributed to it. By breaking a large-scale moral fact into these tiny splinters or fragments, we effectively de-moralize our world. Looking at each action individually, detached from the connections which would reveal its deeper meanings, we see nothing in each such act to condemn or to praise. We refuse to look at how it paves the way for the atrocity it leads to, and we exonerate it from all responsibility. Needless to say, the same demoralization process can occur with regard to actions that contribute to magnificent, heroic events, when viewed as mere aggregates of disconnected "morally neutral" human actions.

When children want to know about morality, we find it very difficult to answer them effectively, because the matter seems both vast and elusive. We are at a loss for an authority to cite whose credentials they cannot question, and we are likewise at a loss for *unquestionable* ethical principles. Involving their consciences seems not to get us very far, and conducting sessions in "value clarification" seems to succeed only in demonstrating our moral wasteland. Nor can we think of good reasons to offer for being honest, respectful of others, etc., without such reasons sounding shallow and superficial. Yet we are sure that there must be a better justification than the one we eventually settle on.

Lisa wonders how it is she hates lies, when she can't recall a single instance in which her parents told her it was wrong to lie. But a child whose life has *integrity* — that is, whose thoughts and actions are consistent with one another, will resist performing an action incompatible with the rest of that child's life, and in fact will be shocked and disgusted by that which is so out of line with that child's normal practices. She'll no more need parental injunctions to avoid telling lies than she'll need to be warned repeatedly not to cut herself when handling a bread knife.

We see this in the learning of grammar. Children learn the rules of grammar and the practice of those rules, until such rules and practice become "second nature." One doesn't have to think of whether this or that one is about to say is correct grammar or not because one habitually practices correct grammar and deplores grammatical slovenliness. And yet, when occasions arise on which there are good reasons for violating such grammatical rules, one may easily proceed to do so, for the rules are not rigid and inflexible. So too with moral practice: it should develop consistently and form an integral whole in the case of each individual. The unwarranted violation of that whole, of that consistency and that integrity, should be looked upon by the individual himself as a self-destructive violation of his own integrity, and therefore wrong, for such morality to be effective.

Children who come to value their own integrity, and who practice honesty as a consistent portion of such integrity, feel lying to be a rupture of the self, and avoid it much more assiduously than they would if it were simply a matter of fairness (although it may be that too). And children who have learned what reasoning is, so that they can distinguish sound from sloppy reasoning, are not so likely to be deceived as to what is or is not compatible with their own integrity, or with the basic direction of their lives. It is for this reason that the learning of reasoning is essential to morality. It is not that children who study reasoning are then able to use their logical skills to settle their quarrels with one another and with their parents, although this may occasionally happen. But what is likely is that such children then have criteria with which to assess what is relevant and what is irrelevant to their interests. They can better judge what fits into the basic scheme of their lives and what fails so to fit in.

We wish to repeat this so as to leave no doubt as to our emphasis upon the point. We do not encourage the teaching of reasoning to children because we believe that moral problems are simply disguised logical problems, which will yield promptly to logical analysis. Such is the glib premise of cognitivists, and we cannot accept it. But we do think it important for adults to encourage children to develop a consistent texture to the fabric of their lives, and they cannot tell what we mean by this until they can appreciate what it is for ideas to be inconsistent with one another, or incompatible, or contradictory. A child can have a life of integrity without learning logic, of course, but logic helps one appreciate the difference between that·which integrates one's life and that which disintegrates it.

We are saying then that children whose lives display wholeness and coherence and integrity are children to whom the distastefulness of, say, a lie, will come as no surprise, insofar as it represents a dismemberment of that integrity. Children whose habits and beliefs have been coherently integrated are the best guardians of their own virtue. If then, we value virtue in children, we should do everything possible to encourage the development of the integrity of their selves.

At the same time, it must be emphasized that the child who is committed to the practice of honesty will shun lying not only as inconsistent with that practice, but as inharmonious with the whole or integrity of that child's life. In this sense, awareness of part-whole relationships is as truly disciplinary in moral education as is awareness of logical consistency. To Lisa, telling a lie would be repugnant, in view of her practice of honesty, in somewhat the same sense that it would be repugnant for her to wear dress gloves with her denims.

Thus the integrity of one's self is based upon an integrity of praxis — one's thoughts consistent with thoughts and actions, and one's individual acts in line with or compatible with the whole character of one's conduct. Unless such praxis has been established day by day, bit by bit, lesson by lesson, moment by moment, into a tough, closely-knit texture, the individual lacks a strong moral base. Such practice is not reducible to a "good reason" for telling the truth, not hurting others, etc. Good reasons are far too inadequate to convey the force of such practice. Good reasons are more likely to come in on those occasions in which overriding situational pressures — something of an emergency — requires that we diverge from what we normally do — and with good reason. It is the exception that good reasons typically justify, not the rule, for the rule is not reducible to a single principle or set of principles. It is the living warp and woof of the interwoven thoughts and actions of the child's life.

The development by the child of such practice is an achievement of momentous importance. Once we fully realize how difficult it is to accomplish, we can have little patience with the superficial slogans which are being offered everywhere in the name of moral education — "letting kids talk it out," "getting kids to see that there's really only one moral value — justice," "laying it on the line to kids — telling them the rules and walloping them if they disobey" — and so on.

To be effective, ethical education must be enormously patient, persistent and scrupulous; it must be carried on in a manner that is truly caring and benevolent, consistent rather than ambivalent, and concerned that children should be helped to think, feel, act and create for themselves. So far, our civilization has devised only one instrument which has even remotely approached serving as such an aegis, and that is the family. Today, with the family under enormous pressure, with its function in doubt and its structure changing, there are efforts to shift its moral function to other agencies, and in particular to the school. Insofar as the school accepts this shift of responsibility, it should be fully aware of what it is taking on. The parent-child ratio was not 1 adult to 25 children — it was between 2 adults to 3 children and 2 adults to 7 children. This gave the family an opportunity to concentrate on moral education at virtually any moment of the day. And if parents have not always been intelligent, they have at least, more often than not, been concerned. If schools now presume to enter the ethical education domain, they must be prepared to enter it on a systematic and scrupulously careful basis — in terms, that is to say, of a commitment from Kindergarten to Grade 12, and with a view to the entirety of the school day, not just a moment during each day devoted to moral inspiration. Such a commitment will in turn require an obligation to neutrality and non-indoctrination on the one hand, and to strenghening the child's efforts at logical, creative, and moral practice on the other. We see philosophy for children as the opening wedge of that commitment.

A final word of caution regarding the relationship of logic to moral education. We have stressed the importance of consistency between one's beliefs and one's actions, as well as among one's beliefs and among one's actions. We have argued that the logic component of the philosophy for children program can be helpful in arousing in children an awareness of the criteria for such consistency, so as to mold more consistent habits and dispositions. And we have contended that the philosophy for children program alerts children to the importance of good reasons in justifying their beliefs, and in justifying departures from patterns of conduct they might normally have adopted.

But there is always the danger that one or another of these elements will be taken out of context and overemphasized. We see a role for logic to play in helping children sort out and understand their own activities, even to the point of recognizing how some of the things they do can undermine their intentions and actions in other respects. But this is not to conceive of logic as a technique for decision-making, as if one need only feed the data into the mechanism and the right answers will automatically pop out. To do so is seriously misleading. Some years ago, for example, we held a series of discussions with some high school students about the usefulness of philosophy, and in the course of one of the discussions, we presented a perhaps overly rosy view of the possible benefits of logical reasoning. As it happened, the students were at that moment engaged in a heated debate over the policy to be adopted with regard to the presence or absence of drugs at the annual class encampment. To our surprise, there was an attempt to press the syllogism into service, as though *it* alone could demonstrate conclusively that certain policies were the right ones. When we endeavored to point out that one could examine the logic of any argument, but that logic *alone* wouldn't solve their problem, the students were rather miffed, as if they had first been oversold and then betrayed.

You should try to avoid similar misunderstandings among your own students — and you can take the most effective step towards this end by being clear in your own mind about the limited usefulness of any one of the components of the philosophy for children program in the absence of the program as a whole. Logic is only one part of philosophy, as moral education is only one aspect of education. As a teacher you should keep in mind not just the relation of logic to ethics, but the relation of philosophy in its entirety to the total educational process — just as you should keep in mind what that total educational process can do for the whole of the child's life.

9. THE IMPROVEMENT OF MORAL JUDGMENT

The problem of how to improve the moral judgment of the young is as complex as any that a society must cope with. That parents should normally have the responsibility for dealing with the problem is of course part of the burden they assume in choosing to be parents. But teachers can rightly be apprehensive about being asked to assume even a portion of such a burden.

Of course, there is no lack of advice. There are experts aplenty when it comes to specifying ways of making children moral. There are those who would indoctrinate and those who would not, those who hold that there are moral principles and those who hold that there aren't, those who favor the development of "moral feelings," "moral character," "moral intuition," "moral sense," and those who decry such efforts as useless. Teachers thus find themselves in a most uncomfortable situation, with social pressure being exerted on them to guide the development of moral judgments among their students, while the pedagogy that would supposedly enable them to perform such guidance turns out in fact to be a chaos of conflicting theories and pseudotheories.

Moreover, while none of the proposed approaches for developing excellence of moral judgment among children has appeared persuasive to the bulk of those concerned, neither has any of these approaches been shown to be totally unworthy of consideration for at least one or another aspect of the matter. It has not been shown, for example, that habit formation is irrelevant, that rules and principles are irrelevant, that aesthetic considerations are irrelevant, that logic is irrelevant, that affective components are irrelevant, and so on. Nor is it likely that any such demonstration of irrelevance will be forthcoming.

Consequently, teachers are being left with the task of deciding which of these many approaches to employ or emphasize, and in what

168

fashion. It should be evident that teachers are going to need a good deal more guidance than they have heretofore been given, if they are to deal effectively with a problem as vast and as bewildering as is involved when a moral dimension is explicitly introduced into the educational process. The philosophy for children approach, in this respect, can be helpful.

To interpret the ethical component of philosophy for children as merely an effort to strengthen children's cognitive powers or *reason* (so that their reason can dominate their emotions) would be to distort our approach enormously. Even if we were to hold (which we most certainly do not) that reason is somehow civilized while human emotions are somehow primitive and barbaric, the notion that reason is some kind of equipment by which emotions can be tamed and dominated is virtually worthless. The image of the rational thinker coolly keeping his head and making perfect deductions while emotions swirl all about him is a vestige of a psychology that should have been recognized as obsolete long ago.*

One of the most perceptive of classic philosophers put the matter quite succinctly when he observed that it is not by reason that a passion can be conquered, but by another and still stronger passion. From which it follows that what should be encouraged in children — if we wish to help them control their inclinations to irrationality — is their impulse to rationality, their natural love of meaning, their desire for understanding, their feeling for wholeness, and their passion for

---

*It may be noted here that while *psychologies* came into being and die out as they are replaced by superior psychological theories, the same cannot be said of philosophies in general, or of ethical philosophies in particular. Psychologies come and go — philosophies remain as permanently possible frameworks of interpretation. The ethical theories of Kant and Bentham, for example, appear several thousand years after the ethical theory of Aristotle, but one cannot say that the later theories are necessarily better than the earlier one. Scientific theories, on the other hand, do succeed each other and replace each other whenever the later can demonstrate its superiority to the earlier. It is therefore a matter of some oddity that some psychologists who are now beginning to tread upon the terrain of ethics naively assume that ethics must be developmental in the way that their own psychological theories are successive and developmental. They even invent elaborate, self-certifying theories of "moral development," in which they demonstrate that children naturally grow up to have moral notions much like those advocated by the psychologists themselves. One can obviously amass considerable evidence in support of such a contention; as a theory of value it is manifestly of little worth, and at each of the so-called "stages," there exists the possibility of mature ethical conduct side by side with less responsible types of conduct. Yet all of these are lumped together as if they were indistinguishable. Thus, for example, the proponents of stage theory offer us no effective means of distinguishing between such conduct as selfishness and self-love, although the moral value to be imputed to such conduct differs enormously. As a result, the net pedagogical effect of stage theory is to confuse and misguide teachers rather than illuminate them as to the proper role they may assume in moral guidance of their students.

investigating the endless byways of their own consciousness. The current flurry of interest among philosophers in the notion of "rational passions" is a healthy antidote to the morbid and futile effort to strengthen the intellect at the emotions' expense.

Indeed, nothing would seem to be more evident than the educability of the emotions — yet few things are so hotly disputed. It would appear that the first order of business in moral education would attend precisely to this point, for if passions are susceptible to cultivation so as to become more rational, then this should indeed be the primary objective of moral education, rather than child-obedience training in respect for so-called "universal moral truths," or teaching children something so indefeasibly cerebral and cognitive as "critical thinking."

That our feelings and desires and appetites do in fact become more sensitive, more knowing, more selective — in short, more judicious — would seem to be difficult to deny. It is not our "minds" that compel our always raw, untutored desires to prefer better works of art, better friends, better jobs, nobler deeds — it is rather the growing judiciousness of our desires themselves. If we would have children prefer noble actions to ignoble ones, we would do well to devote ourselves to the cultivation of their developing tastes and preferences, and to the guidance of their budding appetites and desires, instead of merely belaboring them with moral advice. If we can help children desire more intelligently, have more cultivated tastes and appetites as well as more rational preferences, we will accomplish far more towards making them moral beings than if we merely equip them with a smattering of logic, exhort them to love or respect one another, and induce in them a docile attitude towards our favorite doctrines and ideologies.

The cultivation of children's moral dispositions and the improvement of their moral judgment should be an expected result of our provoking them in a variety of ingenious and surprising ways to the exercise of such of their natural powers as taste, discrimination, reflection and analysis in the countless forms and phases of making, saying and doing. But teachers nonetheless need to have spelled out for them the basic distinction between what it is appropriate for them to do, and what it is proper for them to refrain from doing, with respect to advancing the moral growth of the student. It is particularly useful, in this respect, for teachers to grasp the distinction between the procedural and the substantive, and so to exhibit that grasp that their students will likewise acquire it and utilize it in their own deliberations.

We have elsewhere noted the particular usefulness of the distinction between substantive and procedural considerations with respect to classroom instruction. The teacher, we have pointed out, should normally be neutral when moderating discussions among students about specific substantive issues in which value questions predominate. But the teacher in such discussions should definitely be partial to and insistent upon the rules of procedure by which the discussion is carried on. Should these rules happen to become themselves the substance of the discussion, then the teacher should endeavor once again to assume a neutral attitude towards them. For example, the teacher may make a practice of limiting the amount of time allowed for an individual student's contribution to a discussion. But this practice may be criticized by the class, and become a matter for philosophical discussion — in which case, it would seem, the time-limitation should be suspended until the issue is resolved.

We have also observed elsewhere that it is unrealistic to expect judicious moral conduct from children who are uncaring or morally unconcerned. Now the primary focus of care in a person exercising moral judgment is on procedural rather than on substantive matters. Moral judgment is careful, scrupulous judgment — its opposite is carelessness, lack of attention to procedures because procedures are considered unimportant. Adequate moral judgment therefore manifests itself in care for the procedural principles of inquiry, rather than in insistence upon the rightness of this or that substantive principle of morality. There is an enormous difference between allegiance to, say, *justice* as a substantive principle of moral conduct, and allegiance to fair, non-discriminatory procedures in the resolution of disputes. Unless there is care for the means or instruments necessary for the implementation of justice, we can rest assured that justice will not be implemented. Nor is it fair of us to hold children responsible, when we have never shown them how to be attentive towards the procedures which moral conduct involves.

But if care and concern for procedures are among the objectives of philosophy for children, then it is obvious that the objectives of the program are not limited to purely cognitive matters. Care and concern are primarily affective and character dependent. They are, moreover, quite evidently the result of continual practice and habit-formation. There is in all education a balance between discovery and instruction, freedom and discipline, order and innovation, practice and creativity, and to these there must be added the balance between procedure and substance. It is far better to be clear about the domain of the teacher's neutrality and the domain of unneutrality, about the region of student independence and the region of routine learning, than to be permanently confused about the differences between these contexts, and about the criteria for distinguishing between them.

What philosophy for children can best do is improve moral judgment by developing in children the techniques involved in the making of such judgments, and by developing in them at the same time the love of and the care for such techniques. The capacity of the average person to be consistently judicious in moral matters is highly precarious. Our critical dispositions are easily deflected by self-interest, and our foresight regarding the untoward consequences of our actions is readily blinded by wishful thinking. It is indeed remarkable how persons of character, normally scrupulous in adhering to proper procedures of moral inquiry, can casually ignore considerations of the greatest gravity for other persons involved, should their own advancement be at stake. It is not so much callousness as fecklessness which marks the morally injudicious person — not inconsiderateness towards persons so much as disrespect for procedures. We can inveigh endlessly to such individuals about the need for interpersonal respect, but such exhortations are likely to be no more relevant today than the edifying essays of our more puritanical ancestors.

Indeed, attention to procedure, become part and parcel of the child's character, will do more to develop that child's moral judgment than all the edifying discourses ever written. But at the same time, we must bear in mind that the infinitely varied nuances and subleties of human intercourse cannot be conveyed didactically. Only literature has shown the delicacy and flexibility needed to penetrate and communicate the many-layered multiplicity of human relationships. Consequently the improvement of moral judgment will require for its effectiveness the construction of a special body of literary works that will embody and display the modes of moral awareness, the nature of moral integrity, the techniques of moral inquiry and the alternative structures of ethical understanding. Philosophy for children, to be an effective curriculum for ethical education, must consequently stress the conjoint employment of literary texts, together with philosophical procedures aimed at developing logical proficiency, aesthetic sensitivity, epistemological insight and metaphysical comprehension. Children who care about such procedures are children whose moral judgment is most likely to be improved in the course of their education.

References

Adams, Paul. *Children's Rights: Toward the Liberation of the Child.* Introduction by Paul Goodman. (New York: Praeger Publishers, 1971)

Aiken, H.D. "The Concept of Moral Objectivity," in *Morality and the Language of Conduct*, H.N. Castaneda and G. Naknikian, editors. (Detroit: Wayne State University Press, 1963)

Ashton-Warner, Sylvia. *Teacher.* (New York: Simon and Schuster, 1963)

Arnstine, D. *Theory of Knowledge and Problems of Education.* (Urbana: University of Illinois Press, 1969)

Atkinson, R.F. "Instruction and Indoctrination," in *Philosophical Analysis and Education.* (London: Routledge and Kegan Paul, 1965)

Beardsley, Monroe. *Practical Thinking.* (New Jersey: Prentice Hall, 1945)

Beardsley, Monroe C. *Thinking Straight,* 3rd ed. (New Jersey: Prentice Hall)

Beardsley, Monroe C. and Beardsley, Elizabeth L. *Invitation to Philosophical Thinking.* (N.Y.: Harcourt, Brace and Jovanovich 1972)

Benjamin, Martin. "Can Moral Responsibility Be Collective and Non-distributive?" *Social Theory and Practice.* Fall, 1976.

Bender, Lauretta. *Aggression, Hostility and Anxiety in Childhood.* (Springfield, Illinois: Thomas, 1953)

Bettelheim, Bruno. *Love is Not Enough.* (Glencoe, Illinois: The Free Press, 1952)

Bettelheim, Bruno. *The Uses of Enchantment.* (New York: Knopf, 1976)

Bruner, Jerome S. *On Knowing: Essays for the Left Hand.* (New York: Atheneum Publishers)

Bruner, Jerome. *The Process of Education.* (Cambridge: Harvard University Press, 1960)

Buber, Martin. *Between Man and Man.* (New York: The Macmillan Company, 1965)

Carbone, Peter. "Reflections on Moral Education," *Teachers College Record* LXXI (May, 1970)

Cochrane, Donald. "History of Moral Education Movement in California." In press.

Cochrane, Donald. "Moral Education — A Prolegomenon" *Theory Into Practice.* Volume XIV, No. 4, October, 1975.

Cohen, Morris, and Nagel, Ernest. *An Introduction to Logic and Scientific Method.* (New York: Harcourt, Brace and World, 1934)

Coles, Robert. *Children of Crisis: A Study of Courage and Fear.* (Boston: Little, Brown and Company, 1967)

Dearden, R.F., Hirst, P.H. and Peters, R.S. *Education and the Development of Reason.* (London: Routledge and Kegan Paul, 1972)

Dewey, John. *Art as Experience.* (Minton, Balch and Company, 1934)

Dewey, John. *Democracy and Education.* (New York: Macmillan, 1944)

Dewey, John. *Experience and Education.* (New York: Macmillan, 1938)

Dewey, John. *Experience and Nature.* (New York: W.W. Norton Company, 1929)

Dewey, John. *Human Nature and Conduct.* (New York: Henry Holt and Company, 1922)

Dewey, John. *Logic: The Theory of Inquiry.* (New York: Henry Holt, 1938)

Dewey, John. *The Child and the Curriculum.* (New York: Macmillan, 1955)

Dewey, John. *Theory of the Moral Life.* (New York: Holt, Rinehart and Winston, 1908)

Dewey, John. *Theory of Valuation.* (Chicago, University of Chicago Press, 1939)

Doyle, J. *Educational Judgments.* (London: Routledge and Kegan Paul, 1972)

Durkheim, Emile. *Moral Education.* (Glencoe, Ill.: Free Press, 1961)

Dworkin, Martin S. *Dewey on Education.* Selections. (New York: T.C. Press, 1959)

Erikson, Erik H. *Childhood and Society.* (New York: W.W. Norton and Company, 1950)

Erikson, Erik. "The Golden Rule in the Light of New Insight." *Insight and Responsibility.* (New York: W.W. Norton and Company, 1964)

Evans, Clyde. *Critical Thinking and Reasoning: A Handbook for Teachers.* (New York: Board of Regents of State University of N.Y., 1976)

Evans, Clyde "Critical Thinking: An Ally to Parental Values." In press.

Evans, Clyde. "Facing Up to Values." In *Teacher,* December, 1974.

Evans, Clyde. "Philosophy in the Elementary School." *Metaphilosophy.* Volume 7, #1, January, 1976.

Evans, Clyde. "On Teaching Values, Some Practical Points of Theoretical Importance."

Foot, Philippa R. "When Is a Principle a Moral Principle?" *Proceedings of the Aristotelian Society,* Supplementary Volume, 1954.

Furth, Hans. *Piaget for Teachers.* (New Jersey: Prentice Hall, 1970)

Glossop, Ronald. *Philosophy: An Introduction.* (Delta Book 1974)

Goodman, Paul. *Compulsory Mis-education.* (New York: Horizon Press, 1964)

Goodman, Paul. *Growing Up Absurd.* (New York: Random House, 1960)

Groethuysen, Bernard. "l'Enfant et le metaphysicien." *Deucalion,* II (1947)

Gutek, Gerald L. "Philosophy for Children." *Phi Delta Kappan.* April 76

Haas, Hope J. "Philosophical Thinking in the Elementary Schools: An Evaluation of the Education Program Philosophy for Children." Institute for Cognitive Studies, Rutgers University, 1976. (mimeographed copies, unpublished)

Hall, Robert, and Davis, John. *Moral Education in Theory and Practice.* (Buffalo, New York: Prometheus Books, 1975)

Hare, R.M. "Adolescents into Adults," in *Aims in Education: The Philosophic Approach.* T.H.B. Hollins, editor. (Manchester: Manchester University Press, 1964)

Hare, Richard M. *Freedom and Reason.* (London: Oxford Univ Press, 1964)

"The Rights of Children," a special issue of the *Harvard Educational Review.* Volume 43, Number 4, November, 1973.

Herndon, James. *The Way It Spozed to Be.* (New York: Simon and Schuster, 1968)

Hirst, Paul H. (ed.) *Knowledge and the Curriculum.* (London: Routledge and Kegan Paul, 1974)

Hunkins, Francis. *Questioning Strategies.* (Boston: Allyn and Bacon)

Isaacs, Susan. *Intellectual Growth in Young Children.* (New York: Harcourt, Brace and World, 1931)

James, William. *Essays in Radical Empiricism.* (New York: Longmans, 1922)

James, William. *Talks to Teachers on Psychology: And to Students on Some of Life's Ideals*. (New York: Henry Holt and Company, 1898)

Jaspers, Karl. *Way to Wisdom: An Introduction to Philosophy*. Translated by Ralph Mannheim. (New Haven, Yale University Press, 1954)

Kohlberg, Lawrence. *Stages in the Development of Moral Thought and Action*. (New York: Holt, Rinehart and Winston, 1970)

Langford, Glenn and O'Connor, D.J. *New Essays in the Philosophy of Education*. (London: Routledge and Kegan Paul, 1973)

Levit, Martin. *Curriculum*. (Urbana: University of Illinois Press, 1971)

Lipman, Matthew. *Harry Stottlemeier's Discovery*. (New Jersey: IAPC, 1974)

Lipman, Matthew. *Lisa*. (New Jersey: IAPC, 1976)

Lipman, Matthew. "Philosophy for Children," *Metaphilosophy*. Vol. 7, No. 1, January 1976.

Lipman, Matthew. "Philosophy is also for the Young — At Least Possibly." *The New York Times* (News of the Week in Review, October 20, 1974)

Lipman, Matthew. *What Happens in Art.* (New York: Irvington Publishing Co., 1967)

Lipman, Matthew. *Discovering Philosophy*. 2nd ed. (Englewood Cliffs, N.J.: Prentice Hall, 1977)

Lipman, Matthew, and Sharp, Ann M. *Instructional Manual to Accompany Harry Stottlemeier's Discovery*. (New Jersey: IAPC, 1975)

Lynd, Helen Merrill. *On Shame and the Search for Identity*. (New York: Science Editions, Inc., John Wiley & Sons, Inc. 1966)

Massialas, Byron, and Zevin, Jack. *Creative Encounters in the Classroom*. (New York: John Wiley and Sons, 1967)

Matthews, Gareth B. "On Talking Philosophy with Children," *Royal Institute of Philosophy* Lecture, November 28, 1975.

Matthews, Gareth B. "Philosophy and Children's Literature," *Metaphilosophy,* Volume 7, No. 1, 1976.

Mead, George Herbert. *Mind, Self and Society*. Introduction by Charles W. Morris, ed. (Chicago: University of Chicago Press, 1934)

Mead, George Herbert. *Movements of Thought in the Nineteenth Century*. (Chicago: University of Chicago Press, 1936)

Mead, George Herbert. *Selected Writings*. Introduction by Andrew J. Reck, ed. Library of Liberal Arts, No. 177. (New York: Bobbs-Merrill Company, 1964)

Mead, George Herbert. "The Child and His Environment." *Transactions of the Society for Child Study,* Vol. 3, No. 1 (April, 1898) pp. 1-11.

Mead, George Herbert. "The Relation of Play to Education." *University Record*, Vol. 1, No. 8, May, 1896, pp. 141-45.

"The Philosophy of Moral Education," *The Monist* (Special Issue) Volume 58, No. 4, Oct. 1974.

Montefiore, Alan. "Moral Philosophy and the Teaching of Morality." *Harvard Educational Review*, XXXV (Fall, 1965)

Montessori, Maria. *The Montessori Elementary Material*. (Cambridge: Bentley, 1964)

Montessori, Maria. *Spontaneous Activity in Education*. (New York: Schocken Books, 1964)

Montessori, Maria. *The Secret of Childhood*. (New York: Longmans, Green and Co., 1936)

"Philosophy for Kids." *Newsweek* (September 20, 1976)

Opie, Iona and Peter. *The Lore and Language of School Children.* (New York: Oxford, 1959)

Oscanyan, Frederick S. "A Critical Look at Harry Stottlemeier's Discovery." *Journal of Moral Education.* Forthcoming.

Peters, R.S., ed *The Concept of Education.* (London: Routledge and Kegan Paul, 1967)

Peters, R.S. *Reason and Compassion.* (London: Routledge and Kegan Paul, 1973)

Piaget, Jean. *Language and Thought of the Child.* (Cleveland, Ohio: World Publishing Company, 1959)

Piaget, Jean. *Judgement and Reasoning in The Child.* (Totowa, N.J.: Littlefield and Adams Company, 1928)

Piaget, Jean. *Play, Dreams and Imitation in Childhood.* (New York: W. W. Norton and Company, 1951, 1962)

Piaget, Jean. *The Birth of Logical Thinking from Childhood to Adolescence.* (New York: Basic Books, 1958)

Piaget, Jean. *The Child's Conception of the World.* (New York: Harcourt, Brace and World Inc., 1929)

Piaget, Jean. *The Early Growth of Logic in the Child.* (London: Routledge and Kegan Paul, 1964)

Piaget, Jean. *The Moral Judgement of the Child.* (New York: Harcourt, Brace and World, Inc. 1932)

Piaget, Jean. *The Origins of Intelligence in Children,* translated by M. Cook. (New York: International University Press, 1952)

Piaget, Jean. *To Understand is to Invent: The Future of Education.* (New York: Viking Press, 1975)

Postman, Neil and Weingartner, Charles. *Teaching as a Subversive Activity.* (New York: Delacorte, 1969)

Quinton, Antony. "Logic for Little Americans," *The Times Literary Supplement,* April 4, 1975.

Ribble, M. *The Rights of Infants.* (New York: Columbia University Press, 1943)

Rich, John Martin. "Teaching the Justifications for the Moral Life." *Educational Theory* LXV (October, 1964)

Ryle, Gilbert. *The Concept of Mind.* (New York: Barnes and Noble, 1949)

Salmon, Wesley C. *Logic.* 2nd ed. (New Jersey: Prentice Hall, 1963)

Sanders, Norris M. *Classroom Questions: What Kinds.* (New York: Harper and Row, 1966)

Sarason, Seymour. *The Culture of the School and the Problem of Change.* (Boston: Allyn and Bacon, 1971)

Scheffler, Israel. *Conditions of Knowledge.* (Glenview, Ill.: Scott Foresman, 1965)

Scheffler, Israel. *Reason and Teaching.* (London: Routledge and Kegan Paul)

Snook, I.A. "Teaching Pupils to Think." *Studies in Philosophy and Education.* Volume VIII, No. 2, Fall, 1973.

Taba, Hilda. *Dynamics of Education.* (New York: Harcourt, Brace and World, 1932)

Taba, Hilda. "The Problems in Developing Critical Thinking," *Progressive Education* 28 (November 1950)

Toulmin, Stephen. *An Examination of the Place of Reason in Ethics.* (Cambridge: Cambridge University Press, 1950)

Wheelwright, Philip. *Valid Thinking.* (New York: The Odyssey Press, 1962)

Whitehead, Alfred North. *The Aims of Education.* (New York: The Macmillan Company, 1929)

Wilson, John. *Moral Education and the Curriculum.* (New York: Pergamon Press, 1969)

Wilson, John. *Moral Thinking.* (London: Heinemann, 1969)

Wilson, John. *Practical Methods of Moral Education.* (New York: Crane, Russak and Company, 1972)